Educating
All God's Children

Educating
All God's Children

What Christians Can
—and Should—
Do to Improve
Public Education for
Low-Income Kids

Nicole Baker Fulgham

BrazosPress

a division of Baker Publishing Group
Grand Rapids, Michigan

Published by Brazos Press
a division of Baker Publishing Group
P.O. Box 6287, Grand Rapids, MI 49516-6287
www.brazospress.com

Printed in the United States of America

Library of Congress Cataloging-in-Publication Data is on file at the Library of Congress, Washington, DC.

ISBN 978-1-5874-3327-6

The internet addresses, email addresses, and phone numbers in this book are accurate at the time of publication. They are provided as a resource. Baker Publishing Group does not endorse them or vouch for their content or permanence.

In keeping with biblical principles of creation stewardship, Baker Publishing Group advocates the responsible use of our natural resources. As a member of the Green Press Initiative, our company uses recycled paper when possible. The text paper of this book is composed in part of post-consumer waste.

13 14 15 16 17 18 19   7 6 5 4 3 2 1

In memory of my grandmothers,

Edna Goggin and Louise Jones,

who showed me the importance of serving others,
working for justice, and holding fast
to God's unchanging hand.

Contents

Introduction

In the summer of 2009, I arrived on the campus of Princeton University to attend a faith-based conference. This particular gathering highlighted ways in which people of faith, Christians in this case, can work on "common good" issues. I came to the conference to understand how people of faith conceptualize working with the poor, in the hope of further refining the messaging for my relatively new faith-based initiative about public education inequity. After a long, sticky walk in the sweltering New Jersey humidity, I made my way to my hotel room to freshen up and then journeyed to the conference bookstore.

The makeshift bookshop! It's one of my favorite haunts when attending conferences. The event planners set up tables and displays where speakers and workshop leaders—most of whom have written a book on some topic or another—can peddle their wares to the rest of us, who eagerly whip out our cash. As soon as I enter the space, my inner bookworm wriggles its way out; I have to restrain myself from purchasing everything in sight.

Wandering through the series of tables, I began to notice a familiar trend. Having already been on the faith-based conference scene for a year or so, I'd grown used to seeing books on how Christians should engage on a multiplicity of "make the world better" issues: environmental justice, global poverty, hunger, malaria, HIV/AIDS, and human trafficking. But, yet again, I did not see a single book about the vast inequities in America's public education system.

I left the bookstore in a bit of a funk. I caught up with a colleague and boldly declared: "Someone needs to write a book. We need to make a compelling case that motivates people of faith to help close the academic achievement gap in public schools. There's not a single book here that speaks to what we're doing. I worry that people of faith don't see American educational inequity as a common-ground, moral issue that absolutely demands our action."

And that's where this book project began. I started talking with a few friends, coworkers, and ultimately many other allies about positioning the academic achievement gap as a moral, faith-based issue. In the long-standing tradition of "If what you want doesn't exist, then perhaps you should do it yourself," I embarked on this journey.

I wrestled over whether this book should be written from an interfaith perspective, or if I should use an exclusively Christian framework. I firmly believe in the potential of every major religious group to support common-ground issues like public education equity. My work as the founder of The Expectations Project, a faith-based organization helping to improve low-income public schools, welcomes everyone into this movement. Every religion expresses an ethic of caring for the most disenfranchised populations and strives to bring justice to all peoples. Judaism describes this as *tikkun olam*, or "repairing the world." The Muslim tradition highlights collective responsibility, particularly toward the poor and disenfranchised. Religions originating in the eastern hemisphere, such as Buddhism and Hinduism, encourage a strong sense of caring for the most needy.

In the end I chose to focus on the Christian community in this initial book. As a Christian, I can speak personally to biblical principles about serving the poor and working for justice. My relationship with God and personal commitment to follow Christ had led me and sustained my commitment to improving low-income public schools. I understand and believe deeply in the significant power Christianity wields to draw its followers together to right our nation's wrongs and restore fairness where injustice has long reigned.

On a pragmatic level, I also recognize that the overwhelming majority of faith communities in low-income neighborhoods are churches (with a small, although growing, number of mosques associated with the largely African American Nation of Islam). Christians comprise 88 percent of religiously affiliated Americans, with a full 26 percent defining themselves as evangelical, or born-again, Christians. The numbers and the synergies uniquely exist within Christian communities.

As an African American Christian, I also respect the long-standing tradition of the Black church's role in social justice movements, including public education. While this book calls for Christians to become more actively engaged in eliminating the academic achievement gap, I do not intend to ignore those people—particularly in urban congregations of color—who have long recognized the moral injustices facing many children in public schools. African American pastors, and increasingly Latino and Hispanic clergy, have started public charter schools and private schools, and have pushed for vouchers allowing children in habitually underachieving schools to attend private and parochial schools.

While I applaud these individual efforts to obtain parity for students in poor neighborhoods, we have yet to see a large-scale, coordinated, comprehensive push for public-school equity within urban churches of color. Although this book predominantly addresses communities of faith that are less familiar or less engaged with low-income public schools, I hope that communities of color will embrace these themes and consider how we can further organize to bring much-needed change to low-performing schools.

We need to get busy, and we need everyone to join the movement.

1

A School System Deeply Divided
Notes from Detroit and Compton

I'd just boarded the five-hour flight to Los Angeles, where I was scheduled to speak at a conference. I found my way to a coveted aisle seat, which was next to an older, silver-haired gentleman. After the plane took off he turned to me and smiled the friendly let's-chat-with-random-strangers smile. Returning the nonverbal pleasantry, I took out my laptop nonetheless. Airplane time is precious, gloriously uninterrupted, work time to me. It's time when I'm finally free from phone calls, voice mails, and emails. I always plan ahead and designate specific tasks I want to accomplish on the flight.

"So . . . what takes you to Los Angeles?" my fellow traveler asked. I replied politely, but probably somewhat curtly, that I was traveling "for work." Assuming that would satisfy his curiosity, I turned back to my computer screen.

"Well, I'm going to meet my fifth grandchild. He was just born three weeks ago!" he continued with excitement.

"Congratulations!" I responded. There was a moment of silence, and I thought our verbal exchange had run its course. I was wrong.

"So what kind of work do you do?" he inquired.

Now, as much as I love my work, when I'm pressed for time I don't feel inclined to give my impassioned, five-minute speech about why every child in America deserves a high-quality education, why our country has yet to achieve that goal, and (of course, my all-important crescendo) the three things that you— random stranger—can do to help make that a reality. So I gave him the rather cursory micro-version: "I work to help improve public education for kids in low-income communities, so they can achieve at the highest levels throughout their lives."

Once again I mistook the lull in our conversation as a signal that we were done talking. I began scrolling through my to-do list. But my seatmate wasn't finished.

"Hmmm . . . that's interesting. How did you get into that line of work?" he asked.

I gave another polite and standard answer: "I suppose I've always been drawn to ways that I can make the world a more equitable place, so I'm trying to do that for kids in public schools." I assumed this would satisfy him, so I smiled and shifted my gaze back to the dozens of unanswered email messages in my inbox.

Undeterred, my fellow passenger looked at me carefully and sipped his coffee. "I think," he declared, "you must have a better answer than that. When people are called to work on a problem that huge, something stirs deep in them."

Laughing at his candor and realizing that I wasn't going to get much work done on this flight, I closed my laptop. "Well, yes, that's true," I replied. "But in my case it's a much longer answer." And so our two-hour conversation began. I'm quite sure this dear man heard more about my personal journey than he wanted to know. But he was right about one thing: something (and, I would argue, Someone) had stirred me to do this work. And it started years ago.

The Culture of Low Expectations: Detroit

As my seatmate learned that day on our flight to Los Angeles, I didn't stumble across educational inequity as an idealistic college student in search of a cause. I'd been well acquainted with it since birth. A child of the 1970s and 1980s, I was born and raised in Detroit. My father attended Black schools in segregated North Carolina; my mother was more fortunate to attend integrated schools in Pittsburgh. And they both went to college.

I was born after segregation ended. My parents, like many African Americans of their generation, had great expectations for their children's education. My mother said it was a "whole new world" for us. They believed knowledge, hard work, and a couple of college degrees behind your name were three great American equalizers.

When I was an infant we moved into a three-bedroom, red-brick house on Littlefield Street, which had a mixture of middle-class and working-class families. While most families were African American, there were quite a few Caucasian families as well. Although certainly not wealthy, our neighborhood was reminiscent of that Leave-It-to-Beaver Americana that so many of us long for today. I rode my bike past well-manicured lawns and tall, leafy elm trees. We had annual block parties—a city tradition where families put up white and orange traffic blockades to close the entire street to vehicular traffic. Every parent on our street pooled their resources to set up exciting carnival

3

games. Moms and dads dispensed popcorn and rainbow-colored snow cones to every kid. My parents still have a photo of me taking a pony ride—grinning from ear to ear—during one of those neighborhood parties. My parents engaged in some crafty budgeting to ensure my dad's paycheck stretched to the end of the month, but we had a sense that we'd tapped into a small portion of the American dream.

Three years after we moved to Littlefield Street, my older brother, Jay, was set to enroll in kindergarten, and my parents had to decide where we'd attend school. Since my mother majored in early childhood education during college, she was well acquainted with what to look for when choosing a school for my brother and me. According to my mom, she and my dad knew early on that they wouldn't send us to the neighborhood school. "The teachers were doing their best, but the classes were overcrowded and the students weren't really challenged," my mother said. "Your dad and I worried that all the effort we'd put into preparing you and Jay for school would be wasted."

My mother chose to be a stay-at-home parent. She put a high value on devoting her time to us (which is a choice I now appreciate as a key part of the strong foundation my brother and I received). My father was a businessman with a national shipping company; he was in his late twenties and just beginning to climb the corporate ladder. My mom and dad had to make crucial decisions about our education within the constraints of a one-income family.

My parents explored several school options. They looked into a handful of public schools that allowed anyone in the school district to enroll.[1] Most of these schools had stronger academics than our neighborhood school, but they were miles away from our home. The Detroit area had a number of excellent private schools, but the tuition was beyond our family's budget.

After numerous school visits and intense number crunching, my parents enrolled Jay at Greenfield Peace Lutheran School on Detroit's northwest side, and I followed two years later. A modest parochial school a couple of miles from our home, with relatively reasonable tuition, ensured we could escape from the neighborhood public school. Although it wasn't the highest-performing private school in the Detroit area, the years I spent there—from kindergarten through eighth grade—propelled me ahead of the education most kids in my neighborhood received. Jay and I were fortunate to have those opportunities, and we excelled.

I think it's possible that my brother and I were destined for some degree of academic success because we had two college-educated parents (not to mention a mother who majored in education—and trust me, she had us reading before we even started kindergarten!). I certainly don't discount that, but I've also come to recognize some very tangible differences between my elementary school and my friends' neighborhood public school.

Greenfield Peace had much smaller classes than the public school. Each year I had only twenty to twenty-three students in my class, while the neighborhood public schools had upwards of thirty-five kids in many classrooms. I received much more individual attention because teachers had the luxury to provide it. I could get additional help with skills I hadn't yet mastered. Since the entire school was small, the culture had a personalized feel and a sense of accountability that helped students feel truly valued. That type of culture is much harder (although certainly not impossible) to create at a large public school.

When it came time for high school, our family faced similar choices—but the stakes were even higher. Our once-idyllic neighborhood had fallen on hard times. The economic crisis of the late 1970s impacted Detroit in a dramatic way and spilled into the next decade. As our last remaining Caucasian neighbors moved out to the suburbs, so-called White flight was fully realized in my neighborhood; this meant that all of our local public schools were segregated again, albeit by de facto segregation.[2] Although our community retained some working-class and middle-class families, overall poverty increased as more and more families relied on public assistance.

While all the parents in our neighborhood still wanted the best for their children, our local public high school was woefully overcrowded, the dropout rate increased, and—on average—students' academic performance significantly lagged behind that of students in suburban schools.

Detroit did have two excellent public high school options: Renaissance High School and Cass Technical High School. Both schools required exemplary scores on a competitive entrance exam, excellent middle school grades, and laudatory teacher recommendations. Thousands of children applied annually for only a few hundred spots. Gaining admission to either school was akin to winning the lottery for Detroit parents. Everyone understood that neighborhood Detroit public high schools were nowhere near the high quality of Cass Tech and Renaissance.

I remember feeling tense and anxious as I joined children from all around the city to take the entrance exam. The test administrators led us into a large, dusty, old room at Detroit's downtown public school headquarters. Everyone tried to play it cool—as cool as a nervous thirteen-year-old could act—but we all knew the deal. This test was huge.

Waiting for my admissions decision felt like an eternity—although I'm sure it was only a few weeks. I was quite aware of the impact this decision would have on my family. My parents were in a better position to pay for a private high school by this time, but I didn't want them to. They had paid for my education for nine years, and they sacrificed their own desires and needs to cover tuition. I didn't want them to pay an even heftier tuition bill for another four years.

I have vivid memories of the day I got my letter from Renaissance High School. I ripped open the envelope and saw the first few words: "Congratulations! You have been accepted. . . ." I literally jumped up and down, pumped my fists in the air, and ran around our house squealing like a three-year-old. We got pretty loud on Littlefield Street that afternoon. My brother had been accepted two years earlier (with similar fanfare), so once again we went outside of our neighborhood to get a quality education.

Why was Renaissance so radically different from almost every other public high school in Detroit? I believe the biggest differences were the explicit expectations and the overall culture of excellence. The standards at Renaissance were remarkably high for every student, and we were expected to meet them. Students had to maintain at least a 3.0 grade point average to retain the privilege of being a Renaissance Phoenix (yes, our school mascot was a tricky-to-spell bird of Greek mythology that rose from the ashes). While a 3.0 may not seem particularly challenging, it was no small feat given the mandatory coursework within our rigorous college preparatory curriculum. Every student had to take four years of math, science, social studies, and English, and three years of a foreign language. Our graduation requirements exceeded Michigan's standards and surpassed most affluent suburban school districts. The vast majority of students took physics, calculus, and one (if not several) Advanced Placement (AP) courses.

The teachers, too, contributed to an overall culture of excellence at Renaissance. My gray-haired, slightly goofy, fun-loving

AP biology teacher, Mr. Kline, had boundless enthusiasm for helping us discover why and how nature worked. He accepted nothing less than stellar effort. We threw our hearts and minds into his class. We even went on an overnight camping trip to explore plant life in its natural setting (which was a massive stretch for an urban native like myself). Madame Powell, my trés chic French teacher, pushed me to become a more serious student in countless ways. I spoke fluent French after four years in her class (and I came to believe that you're officially fluent only when you begin to dream in a foreign language). Other teachers, many with PhDs, brought their vast subject knowledge, tenacity, patience, and high standards to Detroit's teenagers.

My high school taught me that academic excellence is contagious. Renaissance High had a unique culture. It oozed from every corner. I spent every day with seven hundred students who all had ambitious academic and career goals. Of course we also had the stereotypical cliques at my high school—athletes, party kids, artsy kids, and those who loved alternative punk rock. But regardless of the group, its members engaged in a constant dialogue about grade point averages, college applications, class ranking, and AP exam scores.

Our teachers fostered intellectual pursuits and rigorous critical thinking, simply expecting us to go to competitive colleges and to be among the best students in the state of Michigan. Period. No excuses. I felt strangely out of place if I didn't bring my absolute best to the classroom every day.

Our school also had an aura surrounding it. Throughout our city we were known as the "brainiacs." Attending Renaissance gave me junior Einstein status among relatives, friends, and neighbors. Even if I struggled to keep up in my classes (and trust me—I had my moments!), everyone else still assumed I was a genius simply because my school address was 6565 West Outer

Drive. Not surprisingly, almost 100 percent of my graduating class went to college. Most of us attended universities that were among the top hundred schools in the nation.

Over the last few years as I've reconnected with high school classmates through social media, I've found myself surrounded by a cohort of overachieving physicians, attorneys, professors, and engineers. Renaissance High's culture of excellence—and, of course, a lot of hard work on the part of every student—propelled hundreds of its alumni to very successful and meaningful careers.

My best friend, Stacey, lived down the street and attended our neighborhood public high school—the very one that my parents had ruled out for me.[3] Stacey and I were inseparable during our high school years. When I wasn't occupied with hours of homework or a host of extracurricular activities (my parents also believed in minimal downtime for teenagers), we spent pretty much every waking moment together obsessing over the hottest pop and R&B tunes, dissecting the latest cute boy on our radar screen, or simply walking to the corner store for a snack: extra-hot barbeque potato chips, Faygo red pop (a Detroit specialty that everyone should experience at least once), and a box of Lemonhead candy.

Even though Stacey and I shared everything, our academic lives couldn't have been more different. Her high school had a notorious reputation: more than half of the students dropped out without a diploma, and violent fights broke out on an almost daily basis. When I was choosing from one of a couple dozen Advanced Placement classes at Renaissance High, Stacey's primary options were low-level English classes and basic math. I can count on one hand the number of kids I knew who graduated from Stacey's school and went on to a four-year college.

One particular memory exemplifies the extent to which Stacey and I were hearing completely different messages during the school day. The summer before our senior year, Stacey and I sat on my front porch blasting the latest New Edition album and singing along with the boy band's current hit.

"I'm so nervous," I whined to Stacey. "I get my SAT scores back in a couple weeks. I took it again, and if I don't get at least 70 points more on the math section, I'm going to lose my mind!"

I distinctly remember Stacey pausing in silence as she turned to face me with a puzzled expression. "Nicki," she asked, "what's an SAT?"

I was shocked and completely silent. Regaining my composure, I carefully described the college entrance exam and why it was so important.

I'd always known that my high school was different from Stacey's, but it wasn't until that moment that I realized we were being educated for completely different life paths. My school absolutely expected me to go to college. But Stacey's school seemed to assume that higher education wasn't in the cards for most of its students. I couldn't understand why my bright, witty, talented friend wasn't considered college material. Even if her parents hadn't fully discussed college details with her, why hadn't teachers or counselors talked to her about college entrance exams or the application process? Wasn't that supposed to happen for every high school student? We both graduated from the Detroit Public School system, but we'd been equipped for two distinct futures.

Straight into Compton

I surprised my family and most of my friends—and definitely myself—when I moved to Compton, California, after graduating from the University of Michigan with a degree in English.

I had seen some eye-catching red, white, and blue banners on my college campus with the words "Make a Difference: Teach For America" and had attended a meeting to learn more about the fledgling teacher corps. My Detroit school experiences had left a lasting impact on me; also I was itching to do something "justice-y." It seemed like a perfect fit. Somehow, Teach For America, this new and untested organization with a Peace Corps vibe, convinced me to pack up my light blue Nissan Sentra and drive from Michigan to the West Coast.

I accepted a position as a fifth-grade teacher in Compton, California. I hate to admit it, but before moving to California my only knowledge of Compton came from gangster-rap artists, like N.W.A., Ice-T, and Dr. Dre. (The 1990s rap songs were hardly a ringing endorsement of the community I would come to treasure; they didn't portray an adequate picture of the culturally rich neighborhood where I would learn some of my most important life lessons.)

A few months after I'd begun teaching, I experienced a déjà vu moment that took me back to the deep truths Stacey and our respective high schools stirred in me several years earlier. Anthony, a raspy-voiced student, quite simply called me out. "Ms. Baker, why are you teaching *here*?" he asked during one of our after-school tutoring sessions.[4] "You went to college," he continued unabashedly. "Um . . . couldn't you find a job anywhere else?" Apparently he'd asked a question that my entire fifth-grade class (and quite possibly their parents) had been wondering. Several students perked up and nodded their heads in agreement, murmuring a chorus of "uh-huh's" and "yeah's."

I vividly remember those words from one of my don't-beat-around-the-bush fifth-grade students. And to be honest, my presence at Stevenson Elementary School wasn't the type of career path chosen by most of my peers. I graduated from a highly ranked university with a degree in English. I considered law school and PhD programs before ultimately choosing to join Teach For America. I'd committed to teach for two years in a low-performing public school. I was working in an economically depressed neighborhood that was notorious for crime and high school dropouts.

I struggled to respond to Anthony's pointed question. "Well, I heard a rumor that the smartest kids in the world were at this school, so I wanted to be here with the geniuses," I said, hoping to reinforce the high academic expectations I had for my students—despite how far behind many of them were.

Anthony looked at me for a moment and then burst out laughing. He was not at all convinced. "Aw c'mon, Ms. Baker, nobody thinks *we're* smart! If they did, they wouldn't give us this broken-down school and these ratty old books. You don't even have enough paper and pencils for us!"

As a first-year teacher, I was shocked that a ten-year-old was fully aware of the implicit disparity in our country's two-tiered public education system. He wondered why someone like me— an African American who had graduated from college and had apparently "made it"—would ever choose to teach in his school. He implied that I had myriad more lucrative, and more worthy, options. Anthony scoffed at the idea that other people thought he and his classmates were intelligent. And he completely understood that his school lacked basic resources and facilities. Most disturbing, Anthony regarded society's low expectations of him as the reason why his school didn't have the necessary supplies. After all, he seemed to suggest, why would our nation bother wasting money on students who weren't smart enough to succeed in the first place?

My wise young student was pretty much on target. He identified the same equity chasm that had pricked my heart a few years earlier when I sat on my front porch with Stacey. Anthony may not have yet grasped the broader complexities of public education in the United States, but he got the basics. He realized that something larger than himself and his own personal ability negatively impacted his education. But Anthony didn't yet fully comprehend that while his education was substandard, millions of children—some who lived just twenty minutes away from his school—received a phenomenal education. Those kids were being prepared for a very different future.

I wish I'd had the language to give Anthony a compelling response. I wish I had been able to give him any response, really. But I didn't. I simply smiled a weak grin and encouraged everyone to get back to work. I prayed that no one would ask me anything else about it. Thankfully, no one did.

But what could I have actually shared with Anthony? What words would reassure my fifth-graders in Compton? They knew something was wrong with their school, even though they weren't likely aware of the broader statistics that haunted me. More than 70 percent of the students in Compton read below their grade level.[5] Fewer than 10 percent of Compton's kids make it to college—and even fewer actually graduate with a bachelor's degree. Compton's dismal academic achievement record and its fiscal mismanagement made it a prime candidate for a state takeover (which eventually happened in the mid-1990s). The state of California had zero confidence that Compton Unified School District could do its job.[6]

I had high hopes and great expectations for my students at Stevenson Elementary, but when I met them in September, their academic performance was no better than the rest of Compton's students. It would have been easy to write them off as another class of future high school dropouts. Most of them read well below the fifth-grade level, and unfortunately their math and analytical skills matched their reading abilities. Almost all their families lived below the poverty line. Most didn't have access to high-quality preschool, which is a crucial building block for future school success. It seemed as if they had been doomed to fail before their first day of kindergarten.

Anthony was right. He was right because I didn't have enough basic supplies for my students, and, like many teachers, I frequently dipped into my meager paycheck to try to make up the difference. He was right because I had Spanish-speaking students join our classroom upon immigrating, but I didn't speak any Spanish. (The district office told me I'd need to make the best of it, because no bilingual resources were available.) Anthony was right because we frequently lacked sufficient working toilets, despite a hardworking janitorial team, and students often had to wait in long lines to use the only functional bathrooms in our school. He was right because barbed wire fences surrounded our elementary campus, and we experienced more than one "lockdown" that year due to nearby violence and police activity. But Anthony was right mostly because it felt as though no one else really cared about any of these deeply entrenched problems.

The Harsh Reality

Growing up in Detroit and teaching in Compton, California, solidified one of my deeply held beliefs: the United States operates two very separate and unequal public school systems. A child's home address typically determines which system she or he will experience. Almost 80 percent of public school students attend the school closest to their home.[7] School choice programs and public charter schools continue to expand, but they still educate a relatively small percentage of students. District regulations and state laws make it difficult, if not impossible, to enroll in a better school across town or in the suburbs. And the difference between two schools, even those in the very same district, is often huge.

The achievement gap is a nationwide epidemic. Every urban center and many mixed-income suburban and rural school districts exhibit significant academic disparities between children in wealthier communities and children in low-income areas. Every state's testing data reveal radical differences between low-income student achievement and middle-class and upper-class suburban student achievement. White students and many Asian American ethnic groups dramatically outperform our nation's African American, Latino/Hispanic, and Native American populations. Consider the following statistics:

- Eighty-three percent of Asian American and 78 percent of White students graduate from high school in four years, compared to 57 percent of African American and Latino/Hispanic students.[8]
- Thirty-seven percent of African American fourth-graders cannot perform basic math skills, compared to only 10 percent of White students.[9]

These disparities ought to prick our moral consciousness to its core. The repercussions of this academic achievement gap are devastating. Taking a longer view, we see that public school inequity means more than contrasting crumbling inner-city school buildings with shiny, expansive high school campuses in the suburbs. It goes far beyond whether or not a school offers AP calculus. It stretches further than the disturbing reality that some schools fundamentally believe all students *can* achieve, while others seem to assume that poor children are destined for failure. What's the bottom line? Public school inequity affects

15

what millions of students are able to do with their lives. Educational inequity profoundly impacts students' futures and, ultimately, their destinies.

Fifteen million children in the United States live below the poverty line. More than half of these kids won't graduate from high school—and those who do graduate perform, on average, only at the level of an eighth-grader. To put this in context, children from wealthier communities graduate from high school having successfully taken trigonometry or calculus. But the average high school graduate from a school in a low-income community is still unable to solve basic algebra problems. High school seniors in middle- and upper-middle-class neighborhoods have successfully deconstructed and analyzed the works of Virginia Woolf, W. E. B. Du Bois, and perhaps even Friedrich Nietzsche. But an urban high school graduate may still struggle to read Harry Potter novels.

If a student graduates from high school with eighth-grade skills, what is she qualified to do? What type of career can she acquire? And if she's lucky enough to be one of the 10 percent of children from low-income communities who attends college, will she be prepared for university-level academic rigor? Not likely.

The educational achievement gap arguably represents the United States' most blatant and chilling example of neglect. America has vast financial and human capital resources. We strive to be the land that provides equal opportunities to every child. But we have let the academic achievement gap fester in poor communities. It overwhelmingly impacts children who are already among our most disenfranchised and vulnerable. For generations, we've allowed millions of children to fall through the cracks. Year after year these students get shortchanged in public schools throughout the country. Simply put, our nation is failing God's kids.

Why Should Christians Care?

My Detroit roots and the years I spent in Compton classrooms deeply influence my passion for eliminating educational inequity. But my Christian principles play an even more important role. I still might have found my way to fifth-graders in Compton, but I've also come to realize how deeply my faith inspires me to help improve public education. My faith, my profound biblical convictions, and my sense of purpose compel me to continually work on behalf of our country's most disenfranchised children.

I remember the day that I made a decision, in my childhood church, to follow Christ. I would be heading off to college in a few months, and my pastor preached a heart-penetrating sermon about the depth of God's love. Weeping, but unsure why, I knew something was shifting. So, as was common in my faith tradition, I took a long walk down the church aisle to the altar. My pastor prayed a brief prayer with me, but I wasn't exactly sure what just took place. (I was also blubbering like an idiot, so my judgment and reason were slightly impaired at the moment.) I sensed a peace that I'd never felt before, and I wanted to understand what caused it.

I started college the next fall, and my faith commitment deepened. As with many, the first few years of my Christian journey included pinnacles, valleys, deep questioning, and moments of complete abandon. But I left college with an unshakable commitment and desire to learn more about the person of Jesus. Above all else, I sought to integrate Christ into every aspect of my life—especially when it came to fulfilling God's mission on behalf of those who have the fewest resources. I had an overwhelming desire to live out Micah 6:8 in my everyday life: "And what does the Lord require of you? To act justly and to love mercy and to walk humbly with your God." I particularly love this portion of the verse from *The Message* translation: "It's quite simple: Do what is fair and just to your neighbor."

And that's still my desire today: to do what is fair and just to my neighbor. I certainly don't get it right every time. God's Word challenges me to examine areas where I can apply that principle more authentically. That said, my faith perspective influences me to naturally view the national disparity in our nation's public schools through the lens of my Christian beliefs. I fully recognize and respect the separation of church and state, but that boundary does not diminish the degree to which my Christian beliefs drive me to do what's fair and just for children in low-income public schools.

Finding the Way Forward

My husband, Alonzo, and I have three children. A fair number of our conversations focus on them, as we articulate our greatest hopes and desires for their lives. Those dreams can range from hoping they'll finally realize the clothes hamper is actually a place where dirty clothes go, to envisioning how our kids might contribute to society's greater good. We want them to have opportunities to achieve everything that's possible and ultimately ascertain God's purpose for their lives.

Alonzo and I don't articulate anything markedly different from what all parents—regardless of their economic situation or educational background—want. I believe all parents hope that their children become well educated, have the opportunity to fulfill their God-given potential, acquire the financial means to make a life for themselves, and, eventually, to have the resources to raise families of their own.

Our public school system does not yet foster that reality for all children. The 15 million children disproportionately impacted by the achievement gap do not have the same opportunities for success and personal fulfillment that other children do. They certainly have the potential, as we'll explore in subsequent chapters. Yet many of these children are stuck in underperforming schools, and too often that potential is stifled before it's brought to fruition.

This book explores how and why Christians have a collective responsibility to ensure that kids from low-income communities have the same opportunities for educational success that wealthier children experience. Regardless of where our own children attend school, Christians should wrestle with determining how God wants us to take care of kids who are left behind in substandard and systemically underperforming public schools through no fault of their own.

My deepest hope is that this book will challenge all of us to wrestle with long-held assumptions about whether or not all children (and by "all" I actually do mean *each and every child*) from low-income backgrounds can actually achieve at high levels. In what ways do our biblical belief systems inform our ideas about the potential of children whose parents are caught in the cycle of generational poverty? What about the young boy brought up by a single mother while his father does jail time? And what do we think of the fifth-grade girl who hasn't learned to read yet or the junior-high boy who immigrates to America and speaks only Spanish? Or suppose both parents work minimum-wage jobs that preclude them from spending time with their children? Do we truly believe all children, if given the right academic resources and support, have limitless potential?

Given the long-standing achievement gap we see in our nation's schools, I submit that our society doesn't fully embrace the idea that all children can achieve. We've consciously, or subconsciously, allowed public school disparities to go largely unchecked for decades. Ironically, most people recognize the need to fix low-income public schools. Every politician laments the unfortunate failings of urban schools; if the topic is broached at a dinner party or picnic, most guests would agree that something isn't working. But far fewer of us are actively engaged in rectifying the problem. As Christians, we are called to fix broken systems and restore what has been lost or been allowed to decay. Sadly, we have little or no voice in the public school reform conversations and debates.

And once we come to grips with our own personal beliefs and mind-sets, what should Christians do? We have tremendous power and potential to build national awareness about educational inequity. We can offer our services (time, talents, and resources) to public school students, teachers, principals, and local community members. We can come alongside parents and community members and advocate for the transformational change necessary to give all children the education they deserve. And as we'll see throughout the rest of this book, we can learn from inspiring and informative examples of how Christians are doing just that. We can embrace and understand their efforts and use this knowledge to spark a public school reform movement in our own faith-based communities.

For the sake of Anthony, my insightful Compton fifth-grader, and the millions of students like him, I believe God is calling us to open our hearts to one of the greatest moral and ethical issues of our generation. I invite us to listen to what God's heart is saying about the most disenfranchised children in our nation, who are full of incredible, untapped potential.

2

Root Causes, Systemic Factors, and Myths

> If you don't understand what the cause is, it's virtually impossible to come up with a solution.
>
> —vice presidential candidate Joe Biden, 2008,
> discussing the origins of climate change

Governor Sarah Palin and Senator Joe Biden went back and forth about climate change during the 2008 vice presidential debate. Debate host Gwen Ifill asked candidates about the origins of global warming: have temperatures increased because of human actions, or are climate changes the result of natural cyclical trends? Palin seemed reluctant to take a firm position on the underlying causes of global warming: "I'm not one to attribute every man—activity of man to the changes in the climate. There is something to be said also for man's activities, but also for the cyclical temperature changes on our planet."

21

Regardless of where one personally lands on this particular issue, I think Biden's follow-up was particularly instructive. Essentially he argued that we have to push ourselves, as best as humanly possible, to research, analyze, and try to understand what's driving climate change. Or, as Biden suggests, if we don't understand the cause, we cannot determine the appropriate solution.

The same can be said for the academic achievement gap. In the previous chapter I made clear the vast academic disparities and inequities that dramatically impact children of color and kids from low-income families. Why do we see such massive achievement gaps? What has led to such enormously different academic outcomes? Before we can reduce the achievement gap, we must first determine what caused it.

In this chapter we will look at the factors and general theories to which most researchers and practitioners attribute the achievement gap. As Christians and other people of faith join the movement to help improve low-income public schools, we should develop a general awareness of why academic disparities exist. As with any issue, different assumptions potentially drive different solutions. If we're going to devote our time, energy, and resources to a cause, we want to ensure that our approach will actually help solve the problem.

If you have the opportunity, I'd encourage you to do a quick experiment. Find ten people, preferably teachers or individuals who work with schools (but anyone will do), and ask them why students from poor families and many students of color, on the average, have lower academic outcomes than their wealthier peers. I'm willing to bet that you'll hear at least five different answers, and likely more.

Unfortunately (or fortunately, depending on your perspective!), we're not going to engage in that larger debate here.

Hundreds of books discuss the origins and root causes of academic disparities. And thousands more journal articles, opinion pieces, and websites have devoted space to the same question.[1] While there certainly isn't universal agreement, the underlying causes do tend to fall into a few broad categories. We will explore how poverty and the history of race and education impact academic achievement. This book does not allow the space to fully do justice to each of these ideas, but we can ground our knowledge in a basic overview of how and why our nation's socioeconomic and racially diverse population have such disparate academic outcomes.

To eliminate the academic achievement gap in the United States, we ultimately will need a multifaceted approach that takes into account a variety of factors that contribute to academic disparity. At the end of this chapter and in subsequent chapters, I promote a particular theory and approach that I believe has significant potential to help all children achieve at high levels.

Poverty

Families in low-income communities disproportionately experience the negative impact of the achievement gap. It's no secret that poverty and lower family income have a direct correlation to less academic achievement. We see the effects of this disparity at every age group, from preschoolers to college-aged young adults.

Betty Hart and Todd Risley's landmark study revealed that, on average, children from low-income families hear 30 million fewer words than their more affluent peers before they are four years old.[2] Hart and Risley's longitudinal research demonstrated a high correlation between three-year-olds' vocabulary size and their language arts test scores and overall school performance at ages nine and ten. On average, students in low-income communities are three grade levels behind their peers in affluent communities by the time they are in fourth grade.[3]

Family income is a big predictor of high school graduation rates and of college attendance at top universities. High school dropout rates are significantly higher in poor communities. The average high school graduation rate in the nation's fifty largest cities was 53 percent, compared with 71 percent in the suburbs.[4] At the nation's top 130 colleges and universities, only 9 percent of first-year students are from the bottom half of the nation's household income distribution, while 91 percent are from families in the top half of the income range.[5]

We know that poverty and lower academic achievement are closely related. But why is the correlation so strong? Throwing out the unfounded notion that children from poor families are genetically less intelligent, let's examine the structural impact that poverty has on some families. How might the circumstances of poverty influence a child's ability to achieve in school?

The Power of Preschool

Our youngest child recently finished two years at an excellent preschool. Prior to enrolling her, I spent a lot of time researching and observing local preschools and interviewing school directors, teachers, and parents. I identified several strong options for our daughter. While one or two of them would have stretched our budget, most were within our family's financial means. And now as a kindergartener, our daughter is reaping the benefits of Ms. Jennifer's engaging, nurturing, hands-on, learn-as-you-play, objective-driven preschool class.

Unfortunately, every parent doesn't experience the same luxury of choice in preschool options that my husband and I did. But every child needs and deserves this type of outstanding preschool education. Poverty severely limits children's access to high-quality early childhood education.

No educator, researcher, or scholar disputes the lifelong importance of an excellent early childhood education. Research studies suggest crucial social, emotional, and cognitive development occurs between the ages of two and five.[6] Therefore, a high-quality preschool experience is more likely to prepare a child for academic success than is a substandard one or no preschool at all.

Most states do not offer universal, free preschool for all children, so parents with greater financial means have better early-childhood options. Parents in wealthy communities may pay up to $25,000 a year for the most competitive preschools.[7] Their children will have a leg up on most children before the first day of kindergarten. Middle-class parents also typically have a range of high-quality options. These parents can choose from among the more affordable Montessori preschools and private independent preschools. These schools can be wonderful options, and their graduates often enter kindergarten either on grade level or ahead of the curve.

Working-class and poor parents, who typically have very limited disposable income, generally do not have the financial resources for high-quality private preschool. These parents are forced to opt for lower-quality preschools (that are often no more than glorified babysitting) or federally funded programs such as Head Start. An early childhood program for families whose household income is below a certain level, Head Start has educated millions of kids in the last forty years. While many Head Start centers and teachers achieve great results, the overall evaluation research indicates that Head Start's comprehensive results are mixed, at best.[8] In many instances, parents do not send their children to preschool at all.

Hunger and Malnutrition

Exhausted after a full day with my students, including ninety minutes of after-school tutoring, I desperately wanted peace and quiet while I packed my things before heading home to grade a never-ending stack of papers. But one student, André, was my "Velcro kid" that week. He just wasn't leaving.

"Ms. Baker? Can I help you with something else?" inquired André. "I've already cleaned the chalkboards and straightened the desks."

"No thank you, André," I said, trying to mask my exasperation. This was the third day in a row that André stayed after school to "help" me.

In a lame effort to get him to be quiet while I finished, I opened my snack cabinet and let André devour a few treats before we went our separate ways. (I'd learned that a few Doritos were a surefire strategy to stop André's incessant chatter.)

After the fourth day of this, I complained to a fellow teacher. "I just don't understand why he's not sick of school at the end of the day. Isn't he ready to go home and play? I can't possibly imagine my class is *that* interesting."

My colleague gave me a sideways glance. "Don't you know his situation?" she asked. "André's family never has enough to eat at home. I think they're trying their best, but he's got at least seven or eight brothers, sisters, and cousins who live with him. He's probably staying around to get some extra food."

I kicked myself for not seeing the obvious signs pointing to André's deeper challenges. From that day forward, I increased my secret stash of snacks for André and anyone else who needed them. In my constant effort to improve my students' reading and math levels and to ensure they were constant learners and critical thinkers, I'd lost sight of their personal realities. While I certainly didn't stop our ambitious academic pursuits, I did become much more aware of their lives. Most of my students were poor, and some didn't have enough to eat. Hungry stomachs clearly added another level of challenge to our classroom.

André's situation is not unique. Children growing up in poverty may have limited access to healthy, nutritious food, or they may come to school hungry. In 2011, Share Our Strength, an advocacy group focused on childhood hunger in the United States, estimated that nearly 16.2 million children go to school hungry. That is almost one in five students. Hungry and undernourished children often cannot learn quickly, and they may struggle to retain information. Furthermore, a lack of nutritious food impacts a child's ability to concentrate and perform well in school.[9]

High-Quality Health Care

Poverty can also impact a family's ability to get adequate health care for children. Many teachers in low-income communities routinely have students who come to school sick or injured because their parents don't have health-care coverage. One of my colleagues had a student come to school with his arm in a makeshift sling. When asked why he hadn't gone to the hospital to get a proper cast, the little boy said that he couldn't go to the hospital because his parents didn't have "papers." (My friend helped the parents find a doctor who would treat their son regardless of their immigration status.)

Rates of asthma and respiratory illnesses are much higher in poor communities, due to heavy air pollution and allergies to things like mold and cockroaches. New York City public schools estimate that asthma prevalence among four- and five-year-olds is more than twice as high among children residing in low-income areas than among children residing in high-income areas.[10] Students who suffer these illnesses are more likely to miss school, causing them to fall further behind academically.[11]

Middle-class and wealthy children with asthma have higher-quality medical care, so they don't miss school as frequently.

Inadequate health care negatively impacts student academic performance. Students who come to school sick or in pain struggle to concentrate and perform at the level of a healthy child. Without medical care, sick children will miss more school and will have a hard time keeping up with their peers.

Tutors and Extra Resources

My husband and I live in the Washington, DC, area. Every spring our local news highlights the competitive college admissions process by chronicling students who do, and do not, get into their schools of choice. My friends and neighbors marvel at how challenging it is to get into the top schools. We have a running joke that in order for our kids to get into a highly selective school, they need to, among other things, earn a 4.5 GPA in Advanced Placement courses, be the captain of a varsity team, start a nonprofit organization, and make a scientific discovery.

That said, many parents in upper- and middle-class communities have the financial means to ensure their children have every advantage in our highly competitive world. I've read about parents who spend upward of $20,000 to prepare their children for college entrance exams and recruit top-notch "college admissions coaches" to help their kids write the most effective college applications. Parents in wealthier communities routinely spend a few thousand dollars every year on tutors, extra classes, expensive educational toys, and academic summer camps.

Poverty limits the ways in which parents can support and supplement their children's education. Parents in low-income communities can certainly find ways to supplement their children's education through public libraries, community programs, and nonprofit organizations, and many families do. But these options dwindle as states, cities, and other privately funded organizations face shrinking budgets during economic downturns.

Tutors and supplemental resources do not determine a child's academic success, but they are a contributing factor that helps students in wealthier communities achieve at even higher levels. I don't think many parents would turn down a private tutor to help their child master a challenging subject. And who wouldn't want the opportunity to send their child to math camp during the summer, if they could afford it? When examining poverty's impact on the achievement gap, we cannot discount a parent's disposable income and ability to supplement his or her child's education.

Some Final Thoughts on Poverty and Education

Given the direct and overwhelming correlation between poverty and the academic achievement gap, some education reform efforts focus solely on family income. The rationale suggests that if we put all of our energy into eliminating poverty and bringing more families out of economic hardship, then we will ensure students and families have the financial resources to spur academic achievement. Some of these same scholars and educators argue that we cannot truly solve the achievement gap *until* we eliminate poverty.[12]

I understand the seemingly insurmountable challenges poverty creates when trying to improve schools for children in poor communities. Poverty appears to negatively influence every aspect of a child's life and community, thus hindering academic progress at every turn. I agree with my fellow educators and reform-minded individuals who believe we should continue to try to counter poverty's impact on America's children. The church can, and does, play a significant role in supporting low-income families through food programs, shelters, and other direct services.

While poverty clearly impacts a child's education, we do have evidence of large-scale, replicable academic success stories in some of our country's most impoverished neighborhoods (which we'll explore in chap. 3). We should be vigilant about providing resources and support systems to help families in poverty, but we cannot use poverty as a crutch for allowing the academic achievement gap to continue.

I don't believe our nation has an imminent or practical solution to completely "solve poverty" in the next few years, as wonderful as that would be. Focusing all of our efforts on reducing poverty minimizes the much-needed concerted effort to improve academic outcomes for children in poor communities *right now*. If we wait to tackle the academic achievement gap, we will continue to lose generation after generation of children to failing schools. We simply don't have time to wait for poverty to disappear. We have to educate all children in spite of their economic circumstances.

Race, Culture, and Language

It's impossible to discuss the academic achievement gap in the United States without exploring race, language, and culture. You may be wondering if I (an African American) am about to explain the academic achievement gap by playing the dreaded "race card."

Well . . . yes, and no.

The achievement gap plays out across racial and cultural lines. It's undeniable. As noted in the previous chapter, Native American, Latino, and African American children, on average, perform below Caucasian children and most Asian American groups. Throwing out the ludicrous, archaic (and, might I suggest, nonbiblical) notion that certain racial groups have superior

IQs, we do need to acknowledge the historical context that impacts the current circumstances of certain ethnic groups. A quick survey of our country's racial history, with respect to public education, reveals that people of color were treated unfairly.

For more than two hundred fifty years African American slaves were not allowed to read or attend school. African Americans endured another one hundred years of Jim Crow laws after slavery ended, which legally relegated Blacks to substandard schools. The 1896 United States Supreme Court ruling *Plessy v. Ferguson* upheld the statute prohibiting African Americans from attending White schools, as long as the two facilities were deemed "separate, but equal." The schools for African Americans were separate—but hardly equal. Black students had inadequate supplies and poor school facilities. African American teachers, while motivated and committed, were vastly underpaid compared to their White counterparts.

A subsequent landmark United States Supreme Court ruling, *Brown v. Board of Education* (1954), finally dismantled Jim Crow laws in the 1950s and 1960s, and African Americans began attending schools with White children. Some White families resisted mandatory, court-ordered integration; many communities erupted with intense violence and overt racism. The first African American children to attend integrated schools endured racial taunting, physical threats, and, in some cases, teachers who refused to educate them properly.[13]

Native Americans have a unique history. The United States government relocated Native Americans to reservations when federal authorities appropriated their land and property. In the 1870s, the government began forcing Native American children to attend federal boarding schools far from their families and their reservations.

The schools were designed to strip students of their Indian culture and language. Students were routinely forbidden to speak any Indian words. Students had to wear traditional American clothing, their hair was shaved, and many students were given new names. The intent, according to many scholars and historians, was to train up a new generation of Native Americans who would readily assimilate into United States culture. In the 1960s a congressional report found that many teachers tried to "civilize" American Indian students rather than educate them. There were also many reports of abuse, malnourishment, and forced heavy labor.[14]

Latino and Hispanic students also faced similar challenges in the United States school system. When Texas became an independent state in the 1830s, for example, Spanish-speaking Mexicans lost political and economic power. In 1870 the Texas state legislature passed a law mandating English-only instruction in all public schools. For the next several decades, low-income Tejano parents were forced to send their children to underequipped, overcrowded, segregated schools. Many schools lacked desks and chairs; most had only dirt floors. Hispanic students received a substandard education, at best.

These conditions continued in many Hispanic and Latino communities around the country until 1973. The United States Supreme Court decided that Mexican Americans qualified as a minority group for school desegregation purposes.[15] Hispanic and Latino students began to attend public schools with White students and other ethnic groups.

As Spanish-speaking populations grow, school districts confront demands for teachers who share the background and home language of the students. Schools have struggled to ensure that students gain English proficiency, while respecting and valuing Spanish language and culture.

I was an African American teacher in a school district rapidly transitioning from African American to what would become a Latino-majority community. I saw racial undertones play out in very concrete ways within my school community.

A delightful student transferred into our school in mid-January. Carlos could have been a candidate for a Gap advertisement, with his large brown eyes, locks of curly black hair, and the dimples that accompanied his shy, but winning, smile. I had been told the previous week that he'd be joining our class, so I created a set of class folders and notebooks for him and moved a new desk into the small group where he would sit with three other students. I was confident that Carlos would slide right into our classroom's groove with minimal effort.

I couldn't have been more wrong.

On Monday morning a school administrator walked Carlos down to my classroom and said, "Good morning Ms. Baker. Here's your new student—Carlos. I'm sure you and your class will make him feel welcome." And with that, she left him at the door and returned to the front office.

Carlos looked around the room. Twenty-eight pairs of eyes stared back at him. Our neighborhood was fairly transient, so my students were used to seeing new kids from time to time—but they still possessed typical fifth-grade curiosity.

I attempted to break the ice by saying cheerfully, "Carlos! Welcome to fifth grade at Stevenson! We're so glad you came to join our class. Why don't you get settled in that empty desk with group three? We'll get to know you a bit more before recess!"

Carlos looked at me with a blank stare. He didn't move.

The class stared at Carlos and then back at me. So I repeated myself, "Sweetheart—you can go ahead and put your things in the desk next to Alise. Group three . . . in the corner? Alise, please raise your hand so Carlos knows exactly where he should sit."

Alise's arm went straight up in the air. But Carlos didn't move.

After what seemed like an eternity, he finally responded, "*Qué?*"

Now it was my turn to stare. "Pardon me?" I inquired.

"*No hablo, maestra, inglés.*"

I had studied French in high school and Latin in college, so I knew only about six Spanish phrases. And on a good day I could possibly count to twenty in Spanish. But I knew enough to understand exactly what Carlos had just told me. I couldn't believe it! *Is someone playing a practical joke?* I wondered. *I get a new student, and no one bothers to mention he doesn't speak a* word *of English?* I wish my initial internal reaction had been more positive, but I'll admit that I was floored. Fortunately, I was able to muster a smile for Carlos, as I quickly remembered that he was undoubtedly much more scared than I was.

I had three or four bilingual students who spoke Spanish and English. One of them, Daniella, who functioned as the official "mother hen" of our classroom, walked right over to Carlos and started speaking to him in Spanish. Carlos perked up as he and Daniella carried on a full conversation. After their exchange, Carlos hung his backpack and coat in the back of the room. He found his seat next to Alise; he placed a notebook and pencil on top of his desk. Carlos was ready to learn. But I had no idea how to teach him.

During recess Daniella was able to tell me that Carlos and his family recently moved from El Salvador to Compton. He was in the fifth grade in Central America and had done quite well in school. His academic record hadn't transferred to our school, so I wasn't sure what he'd been studying in El Salvador.

I made a beeline to my principal's office and peppered him with urgent questions: Is there a bilingual teacher in our school who could work with him? (No.) Are there any bilingual tutors in the district who might be able to meet with Carlos a couple times a week? (No.) Does our school have any Spanish textbooks or literature books that I could give him? (No.) My principal suggested I call the central office to see if I could secure any additional resources.

My calls to the district office yielded nothing. At that time, schools required a minimum percentage of bilingual students before receiving bilingual teachers or resources. Stevenson Elementary had a growing Spanish-speaking population, but it had yet to catch up to Compton's overall demographics. The city of Compton transitioned very quickly from an African American majority of 78 percent in 1980 to almost 45 percent Latino in 1990; by 2000 the city grew to have a Latino majority (57 percent). Compton's school enrollment saw an eventual 51 percent decrease in African American student enrollment between 1985 and 2005.[16]

Compton's school district leadership remained largely African American as the Latino population rapidly increased. Professed "black and brown" tensions bubbled over in Compton, resulting in demands for more teachers and school officials who shared the backgrounds of the rapidly emerging Latino demographic. Parents protested what they perceived as a lack of support for Spanish-speaking students. Most parents wanted their children to learn English; they demanded more home language resources to help with Spanish to English transitions. Several parents and Hispanic civil rights groups accused the largely African American leadership of not caring about Latino students' needs.[17]

One can argue about the motives of the African American leadership in Compton. Were they overtly racist in their apparent lack of concern for Latino students? Or was it a district struggling to keep up with a rapid demographic shift? Based on my experience as a teacher during that time, I believe the overall district leadership was insensitive, at worst, and vastly unprepared, at best, to meet the needs of this emerging population. Regardless, I believe Carlos certainly deserved to have his academic needs met more quickly. I eventually purchased some Spanish resources for Carlos out of my own pocket. I brushed up on my Spanish in the evenings and was able to hold basic conversations with him. But I was never able to truly provide him with the quality instruction he deserved. I sat him next to Daniella and other bilingual students. They translated for him as best they could, which unfortunately reduced their own instructional time as well.

By the end of the year Carlos was fairly proficient in English (mostly picked up by listening to his friends and, by his own admission, from watching American television). But he'd essentially missed half a year's worth of instruction, so he was far behind the rest of my class. The dynamics of race and racial politics continue to play out for students like Carlos and those who belong to other historically disenfranchised ethnic groups.

How do these disturbing pieces of history, and more recent stories like my experience with Carlos, connect to modern-day achievement gaps between racial groups? Many scholars argue that bias and discrimination, even when subtle or subconscious, impact students of color. Society's indirect messages about which students have the greatest potential can creep into even the most progressive, open-minded, self-aware educator. Teacher bias—against girls, minorities, poor children, or children with physical disabilities—can severely impact a teacher's ability to hold all children to high academic standards.[18]

Racism, language bias, and discrimination don't fully explain the achievement gap, but if we fail to acknowledge the role that race has played and continues to play in our educational system, we're likely missing a piece of the puzzle. We will also be viewed as ignorant or insensitive if we don't bring some awareness of these issues to our efforts to help close the achievement gap. It's almost impossible to ignore racial dynamics when understanding how academic inequities continue to persist.

And, again, the church is in a unique position. While many communities still wrestle with the residue of historical racism or negative stereotypes due to lack of cross-cultural understanding, at its best the church can provide a wonderful example of cross-cultural understanding and courageous leadership. Christians truly have the opportunity to play a role in helping to resolve some of the lingering racial insensitivity and injustices as we work for equity in public schools.

Parents and Families

I often have the opportunity to speak about public education at faith-based conferences and events. I've learned to anticipate the types of questions I'll receive from the audience. One of the most common questions goes something like this: "All those suggestions to improve schools are fine, but we can't control what happens when the kids aren't in school. If the parents truly cared, wouldn't they find a way to get their children to achieve?"

When we are less familiar with a group or culture, it's easy to inadvertently make assumptions about what we don't understand. I think we see this frequently with respect to parents in low-income communities. "If only they cared!" is heard too often from middle- or upper-class individuals. However, after working on urban education issues for two decades, I completely reject that assertion. Contrary to some of society's commonly held assumptions, I've found that almost all parents *do* want the very best education for their children.

That said, I understand and empathize with how easily we can all make assumptions about people in different communities. I certainly carried some of those biases when I began teaching. Although I am an African American woman from a working-class Detroit neighborhood, I lived a fairly middle-class lifestyle for much of my life—which afforded my mother, in particular, the opportunity to be very involved in our school. My father worked outside of the home, and my mother was a stay-at-home parent who volunteered at our school until I was in middle school. She was the annual "room mom" who helped teachers plan parties and activities. My mother chaperoned field trips, organized a Girl Scout troop, and even filled in as a substitute teacher on occasion. She attended every single parent–teacher conference and helped us with most school projects.

My father, who valued our education just as much as my mother did, wasn't able to do many of those things. He was climbing the proverbial corporate ladder, which required traveling to client meetings around the country and putting in ten- or twelve-hour days. He helped with our schoolwork when he could and tried to attend special school events, but he couldn't do those things as consistently as my mom, given the demands of his job. Unfortunately, I didn't automatically apply that perspective to my students' families.

I reached out to my students' parents and families early in the school year, as a part of an overall plan to get my students on track academically. I came armed with diagnostic testing data that, in most cases, illustrated how far behind each child was. I had honest conversations with moms, dads, aunties, and grandmothers about the significant progress we needed to see that year. Each and every family member wanted his or her child to achieve that year. But I quickly learned that the process to get parents and families involved, in a meaningful and productive way, required a different approach.

While all of my students' parents verbalized strong academic desires, I didn't sense their support during our first parent–teacher conferences in early November. Students had the day off so parents could attend one of the thirty-minute time slots between 8:30 a.m. and 3:00 p.m. I proudly displayed my students' work around the classroom and prepared individual portfolios and personalized notes for each parent.

Much to my disappointment, only four or five parents showed up. Devastated and frustrated, I judged the parents who didn't attend. After all, at least one of *my* parents came to every one of my parent–teacher meetings; why couldn't my students' families make the same effort?

As I relearned over the next few months, not every family had the same advantages that I did as a child. I knew this intellectually, but I struggled to remember it while knee-deep in the teaching trenches. I knew my students and I didn't grow up in similar economic circumstances, but I neglected to connect how those differences impacted our respective lives. For example, I realized that many of my students' parents worked more than one job. They had very little free time to make it to a teacher conference during the regular school day. Some parents worked hourly jobs with no paid vacation days. They would literally lose money if they asked for time off (and most employers weren't even required to give them unpaid leave). Three hours of pay may seem relatively small, but it's very important for families who live at or below the poverty line.

Many of my parents or grandmothers were single caregivers, creating an additional layer of challenge. Single parents likely need to juggle intense work schedules to attend a school meeting, in addition to finding child care for any other siblings.

These complexities made it tough for many parents to join me for those November teacher conferences.

I had to create alternative ways to engage my students' parents and families. We held telephone conferences instead of meeting at school; we set up weekend conferences; or we met later in the evening when parents weren't working. The traditional parent–teacher conference approach didn't work, but not because these parents didn't care. Their life circumstances required me to adjust to meet *their* reality. And it was my job and responsibility to do so.

If you are not from a low-income community, I encourage you to spend some time getting to know parents in impoverished neighborhoods. You'll be hard-pressed to find a parent who says, "Oh yes! I really hope my child becomes a high school dropout! That's my goal for her." But let's push our thinking even further on this sensitive topic. What if a parent in a low-income community still doesn't demonstrate action to help her child succeed? Should Christians relinquish our obligation to help the child? Absolutely not! Children cannot be held responsible for their parents' actions. Period. I cannot imagine Christians looking at a starving child in Sudan and declaring, "Well, if her parents would just work harder, they could find a way to get more food. I'm not going to send any money to that relief agency until the parents can do a better job!" Clearly we feel compassion for that Sudanese child, regardless of what we think the parent is or isn't doing. Likewise, we need to extend the same Christian compassion to students in low-income public schools. How can we excuse ourselves from helping any child in need?

Having described some of the unique challenges that some families may face in low-income communities, I'm still the first to suggest parents and families should strongly support their children's schooling. The church can play an important supporting role for families in low-income communities by providing mentoring programs, financial assistance, and low-cost or free child care options. And, perhaps most important, church leadership can use their "bully pulpit" to ensure that parents know how to best advocate for and support their children to ensure academic success.

Pursuing Student Achievement

Poverty, racial history, and family circumstances all contribute to the academic achievement gap in our nation's public schools. If our country is going to provide high-quality public education for all children, then we must pursue strategies that mitigate the various challenges and seemingly entrenched circumstances. Is there hope? How can Christians get involved and become part of the solution? In the following chapters we turn our focus to some encouraging news. The achievement gap can be eliminated, but it will take significant public will, many allies, and a dogged belief in the potential of all children.

3

The Good News

Hard Work Yields Success for All Children

Not restricting my conversations to airplane seatmates or faith-based conferences, I'm prone to discuss public school inequity in coffee shops, at dinner parties, and in grocery store lines. After hearing the problem, my conversation partner inevitably asks, "All right—I understand that a lot of poor and minority kids get a raw deal in public schools. But doesn't this seem like an impossible problem? Is there really anything we can do about it?"

After mentally thanking the earnest questioner (after all, they've completely set up my next point), I then declare my unwavering belief: the academic achievement gap does *not* have to exist in the United States. We have hundreds and thousands of examples of teachers, schools, and—increasingly—entire school districts that successfully narrow the achievement gap each year.

The reaction I receive is typically very positive. It's as if people exhale and exclaim, "Thank goodness! Someone's finally talking about how we can solve this problem!" Conference attendees say that for the first time they're embracing the idea that all children can achieve academic success, regardless of their economic or racial background. I'm convinced that my words and anecdotes are not what ultimately move the audience members. In a time when society's problems appear exceedingly massive and all-consuming, we are all in desperate need of a little hope, and we all resonate with a message that highlights what is *possible*.

As our nation and our communities of faith, in particular, develop greater awareness of educational inequity, it's tempting to get stuck at the "This problem is huge!" stage. But that limits our ability to move forward and fix inequality. We lose an entire audience of people who often walk away believing the problem is intractable. And I can't say I blame them. I cannot imagine why anyone would want to volunteer his or her time on a problem that seems impossible to solve. Why would one contribute time and resources to a social problem that ultimately can't be eradicated? I certainly wouldn't.

That's why an educational equity message bearing "good news" resonates so strongly and has significant power to facilitate deep change. Fortunately, there is a great deal of good news with respect to eliminating the academic achievement gap. Children in low-income communities can achieve at the highest levels. Period. No disclaimers needed.

This chapter illustrates success stories that nullify the myth that children in low-income communities cannot achieve at the highest levels. These stories share common themes about the importance of setting ambitious goals and maintaining high expectations, and about the importance of providing additional resources, human capital, and investment to ensure that students are successful. Most of all, these stories show that change requires incredible persistence in the face of immense challenges.

I considered filling this chapter with a half dozen models of excellence—highlighting phenomenal teachers, schools, and programs that have achieved excellent results. But that didn't feel authentic. The reality is, while hope and good news do exist, success is a long, hard slog that requires dedication, commitment, and many, many laborers joining the movement. So, instead, I focus on my own experiences and challenges in the classroom and then highlight some impressive schools that are accomplishing great things.

My teaching experience forever changed my life and transformed and solidified my belief about what's possible in low-income public schools. No one can ever convince me that it's impossible to turn the tide of academic failure. This work is not easy, but I believe this problem can be solved. And I believe that the Christian community is a vital part of the solution. Before we tackle the hard work, however, let's embrace the good news.

Ms. Baker, Meet the Achievement Gap. Achievement Gap, Meet Ms. Baker.

On a hot, September morning in Southern California, I began my first day as a fifth-grade teacher. I found twenty-eight amazing students waiting for me in my neatly organized classroom with freshly decorated bulletin boards. Full of seemingly boundless energy, my students were abuzz with first-day-of-school excitement.

Other Stevenson Elementary School teachers, mostly veterans with at least ten years in the classroom, teasingly said that I looked young enough to blend in with my own fifth-graders. One seasoned teacher remarked, "Are you sure you can handle this, honey?" I assume she meant well and was speaking out of motherly concern, but I was slightly terrified that she might be right. All manner of thoughts ran through my head that first morning: What if the students don't listen to me? I assumed I'd have kids that were far behind academically, but what if they were *too* far behind? Could I help them catch up in just one school year? And why in the world did I agree to do this?

To be honest, those first few weeks were a blur. I faltered in finding my teacher voice. I wasn't comfortable as the classroom authority. I struggled to convince the class that I was serious about everything I said, including when I stated that homework had to be completed each and every day. I wanted to institute simple things, like pencil sharpening procedures, as well as deeper concepts, such as developing a classroom culture of mutual respect.

As if all of those things weren't enough, my initial diagnostic tests revealed what I'd suspected. Most of my students were extremely far behind. They didn't require a few mere tweaks with multiplication or a short refresher in order to craft a more perfect five-paragraph essay. Their skills were years and years behind that of an average fifth-grader. About two-thirds of my fifth-grade class were reading, writing, and doing math at the second-grade level. An average fifth-grader should be able to read Harry Potter books with minimal effort, but many of my students barely made it through the classic children's picture book *Goodnight Moon*. An average fifth-grader should master long division and basic fraction computations, but many of my children struggled with basic two-digit addition and subtraction problems that required borrowing or carrying numbers from the "ones" to the "tens" place.

Adding another dynamic to the mix, a handful of my students were classified as nonreaders. They didn't know the basic sounds that letters make. I recall several particularly painful moments when those students read aloud in the beginning of the school year and endured humiliating giggles and exasperated sighs from their classmates as they read slowly and stumbled over half the words. And, yes, believe it or not, all of these students were fifth-graders who'd never been retained in previous grades.

As this reality sank in, I also faced another truth. Somehow I was expected to ensure that my entire class was ready for the sixth grade by the end of the school year—a mere nine months away. I felt like I was being handed mozzarella, tomato sauce, dough, and pepperoni and told, "Now, we'd like you to take all this and bake a phenomenal peach cobbler. Good luck!" It felt utterly impossible. I struggled to maintain my deeply held belief that academic success was possible for my students. I so wanted my class to achieve, but when I came to grips with how far behind they were, I began to lose hope that high academic achievement was possible. I had a vision, but I grappled with how to put together a cohesive strategy that would make the vision a reality.

So I foundered. No, I take that back. During those first few weeks, I—quite simply—failed.

In those first couple months I didn't provide my students with anything close to the quality instruction they deserved. I spent hours planning what I thought were fun and engaging lessons, but most of my students talked over me and pretty much ignored what I was saying. As I'd learned in my teacher-training program, I created a system of rewards and consequences to motivate positive behavior, but I didn't follow through on the system in every single situation. Due to my inconsistency, students got frustrated with the system because they thought I was showing favoritism to some students and unfairly disciplining others. Naïvely (and somewhat arrogantly), I disregarded some of the advice and lessons I'd received during training and broke the cardinal rule of teaching: I was overly concerned about whether or not my students liked me. This meant, not surprisingly, that I failed to make the difficult decisions that would have led my class to respect me, which, as it turns out, is far more important than being liked.

When I reflect on my first couple of months in Compton, I can—without reservation—declare that very little learning happened in my classroom. I didn't create an environment that fostered academic pursuits and high behavioral expectations; so my students ran the show. If I didn't find a way to turn the tide, my nonreaders would still be functionally illiterate in June. My students who couldn't do basic math problems would still be unable to correctly count their change at the corner grocery store.

It Takes a Village

The national teacher corps that I joined, Teach For America, brought about five hundred teachers together the summer prior to my first day as a teacher. During that summer training session, I met an exceptional group of young adults, many of whom would become longtime colleagues in the struggle to provide all children with a quality education. Once the summer ended, I rented a house with two young Christian women, Samantha and Danielle, whom I met during Teach For America's training. I honestly don't think I would have made it through my first year of teaching without their friendship, commiseration, and prayers. We built a supportive, intentional living community around our mutual faith and our common first-year teaching challenges.

We shared similar stories during our first weeks in the classroom. We awoke before dawn to beat the Los Angeles traffic and arrive at school well before the 7:45 morning bell rang. Every evening we returned home and flung ourselves on the living room floor, drained of nearly every ounce of energy and every coherent thought. Not surprisingly, there were tears—lots and lots of tears. We each shared daunting stories about the immense obstacles our students faced.

A few weeks into the school year, my class was at an academic standstill. I noticed that Samantha and Danielle were moving up the learning curve faster than I was. They both taught kindergarten, so they shared lesson plans and age-specific strategies with each other. But I also noticed something else. Where my pride prevented me from asking for help (I've always been reluctant to admit I cannot handle things myself), Samantha and Danielle were completely unashamed to ask. If they observed a teacher doing something that worked, they'd ask him or her about the approach. Then Samantha and Danielle would borrow it, photocopy it, make it, or buy it at the teacher supply store. They'd internalize it, practice it, and make it their own. Both of them would replicate a successful classroom management strategy or an effective lesson plan in a heartbeat. They didn't think twice about it.

After the first few weeks of nonlearning in my classroom, I realized I needed to adopt Samantha and Danielle's strategy. Thankfully, an extraordinary veteran teacher worked next door to my classroom.

Mrs. Blackwell, who had been teaching for twenty-five years, was a middle-aged, fashionably dressed woman who taught the other fifth-grade class at Stevenson. I was overwhelmed and on the brink of tears during most of those first months, but she came to school perky and joyous every morning. Our classrooms opened directly into the sunny courtyard, and each morning I heard Mrs. Blackwell's students greet her with a respectful and cheery chorus of "Good morning, Mrs. Blackwell!" as they formed a perfectly straight line in the courtyard. Her students knew what she expected of them, and they got to work right after the morning greeting. She'd skillfully divided them into small groups in which students worked independently on their math and reading goals. The objectives for her lessons were very clear, and she had an even clearer plan to ensure her students achieved them.

Mrs. Blackwell gave her students explicit behavioral expectations; she clarified them from day one. She followed through on consequences for misbehavior, and the kids knew it. Therefore, very few students even attempted to challenge her authority.

In short, Mrs. Blackwell was a highly effective teacher, and her fifth-graders were on track to learn substantially more than my students. She was closing the academic achievement gap for her students, and I was, at best, maintaining the status quo and, at worst, causing my students' academic gaps to widen.

One morning, after a particularly rough lesson (or nonlesson, if I'm being completely honest), I found my way to Mrs. Blackwell's classroom during lunch.

Mrs. Blackwell asked me, "How's it going over there, Ms. Baker?"

I promptly started to cry. I literally sobbed while Mrs. Blackwell discreetly got up and closed her classroom door so no one would witness the broken-down teacher I turned into that day. She put her arm around me gently and waited for me to speak.

"I just don't know if I can do this," I confessed. "I'm trying so hard, but I don't think I'm getting through to my kids. They don't listen to me; they do what they want to all day long! I don't think they're learning much at all. We probably won't get anywhere close to where they need to be by June. They're so far behind! Some of them can't even read. I'm beginning to think this is a complete waste of time!"

"Sweetie, I heard you mention to another teacher that you're looking for a church home in the area," Mrs. Blackwell began. "So can I assume that you're a Christian?" When I confirmed her hunch, she asked if we could pray. Clearly in no position to turn down any help—divine or otherwise—I readily agreed.

And right then and there Mrs. Blackwell prayed for me.

I felt a sense of peace come over me, a peace that I'd struggled to find in those first weeks with my students. I realized I'd found a mentor, a prayer partner, and a surrogate mother all rolled into one.

And that's when things began to turn around for me and my students. We started the long, hard road toward the academic ideals I wanted to birth in September. The deep-rooted belief I'd been carrying regarding what was possible for my students became a living, breathing tangible plan.

During the next weeks and months, Mrs. Blackwell, and a few other cherished mentors, helped me change some things. First, I realized that I was indeed in charge of the class. I had to make the tough disciplinary decisions that sometimes caused a child to (gasp!) not "like me." I had to follow through on behavioral consequences each and every time. While this was painful and tedious in the beginning, I quickly learned it had an unexpected effect: the more I consistently followed through on consequences, the more my students respected our classroom management system—and the less likely they were to misbehave. In addition, the more I focused on rewarding students for positive actions, the more my students sought that positive reinforcement—which reduced many of our behavior challenges as well.

Mrs. Blackwell also encouraged me to build strong relationships with my students' parents and family members. While that required a significant time investment, it paid off in both the short and long term. I shared an academic vision and classroom goals with my students' families. I was brutally honest about how much we needed to achieve that year; every family member was on board to push as hard as we could. Those relationships helped me build alliances and trust with my families. When I called home to discuss a behavioral challenge, the parents backed me up completely.

I remember one young student who enjoyed talking to his friends during class time; he distracted those around him and hindered his own learning. It took only one phone call home for him to straighten up. Even his friends questioned him: "Dang, Maurice, how come you're being so good all of a sudden?" Maurice sullenly responded, "She called my mom." That was it. That's all it took for many of my students. Mrs. Blackwell helped me realize the importance of family connections and how they influence student behavior and learning.

In late November, the veteran teacher who questioned my abilities in September sashayed by my classroom and said, "Well, well, well, Ms. Baker. Looks like you could handle it after all!" I simply smiled to myself and kept on teaching my small reading group. It was already November, and we still had much to accomplish in order to catch up. And as far as I was concerned, we'd barely scratched the surface.

Refiner's Fire

"Ms. Baker—this doesn't make any sense!" an exasperated student blurted out during a lesson on long division in early December. Jamal, a tall, quiet student who rarely spoke during class discussions, was at one of the chalkboards with three other students. Each student had to work through the steps of "divide, multiply, subtract, bring down" of long division, which was still a popular math concept when I was a first-year teacher. Even when a student understands why the various steps are necessary, the process can be confusing to any student—and Jamal was dismally far behind in his math skills. Our September diagnostic tests classified him as having only mastered first-grade math. Yet he was in front of the class trying to pull together a complex math problem that required skills he never really learned in second, third, or fourth grade.

The situation quickly escalated into a full-blown disaster. Jamal slammed his chalk onto the blackboard tray and stormed back to his seat. The rest of the class sat stunned in wide-eyed silence. Soft-spoken Jamal hardly uttered a peep during class, so for him to have this type of outburst caught everyone's attention. Jamal sulked during the rest of the lesson and completely disengaged that entire day.

This represents just one of hundreds of setbacks we encountered during the school year. By the end of October we'd moved beyond traditional classroom management hurdles, but every child didn't experience instantaneous academic miracles. Despite several Hollywood films that neatly wrap up all challenges faced by an inner-city teacher in less than two hours, it takes much longer in an actual classroom. There is no secret to instant academic success.

I liken the process of closing the academic achievement gap to how silver and gold become purified through a refiner's fire. The biblical analogy in Zechariah 13:9 illustrates the often painful and long-suffering process God uses to help us become more like him: "I will bring that group through the fire and make them pure. I will refine them like silver and purify them like gold" (NLT). Just as fire continually distills impurities from gold and silver, God uses challenges and hardships to singe imperfections from our character and habits. Challenging tests and trials push us to become the people God desires. There are no shortcuts for our spiritual and character development.

Similarly, there are no shortcuts to closing the achievement gap. As Teach For America's CEO and founder, Wendy Kopp, writes in her recent book, there are "no silver bullets or silver scapegoats." She says,

> The urgency of the achievement gap makes us yearn for a quick fix that will close it. Yet everything we are learning from the most successful classrooms, schools, charter management organizations, and districts proves that there are no shortcuts.[1]

The path to success didn't appear with a snap of my fingers. When we successfully tackled one problem—like classroom management—another challenge took its place. Then we had to tackle those as well. The process continued for the entire year. Fire—then a little gold dribbled out. More fire—a teeny portion of silver. Still even more fire—and perhaps a larger deposit of silver and gold this time. We continuously strove to narrow the achievement gap, but the scorching refiner's fire, which Jamal illustrated for me that December morning, came in the form of dozens of obstacles that we encountered every day.

I'll admit it: at times I was tempted to float along with the status quo. Jamal, like many students, had been promoted every school year even though he could barely read or perform basic math operations. Why should this year be any different? If I had just one Jamal in my classroom, I could create a plan to fill in his academic gaps by June. But I didn't have one Jamal. I had fifteen or sixteen students struggling as much as Jamal, if not more.

Through tearful and exhausted prayers, I came back to the constant realization that we simply wouldn't make any progress unless we tackled each student's academic challenges directly and applied a goal-oriented focus with unrelenting persistence. As one of my roommates often said during that first year, "They didn't fall behind overnight, so we're kidding ourselves if we think we can snap our fingers and fix these problems tomorrow." I'd signed up for a marathon with my fifth-graders: I simply refused to let them leave my class in June without seeing the finish line. I couldn't change or judge what happened to them in previous school years. I kept repeating a mantra: Not this year. Not this year. Not . . . This . . . Year . . .

Maintaining that perspective helped me view each challenge as an opportunity. Every struggle taught me an important lesson that propelled us forward. We weren't going to become successful scholars if I didn't help guide my students, and myself, through the growth process.

Above and Beyond

Time on Task

When Jamal completely disengaged from that long division lesson, his frustration forced me to realize one of my most important lessons that year. As I talked to Jamal I discovered that he had never learned basic multiplication and division facts (e.g., "six times seven equals forty-two" or "fifty-six divided by eight equals seven"). Students typically understand and memorize those facts in second and third grade, so it was almost impossible for him to successfully tackle the complex steps of long division.

I related Jamal's struggles to Mrs. Blackwell and my Teach For America mentors. We quickly came to the conclusion that Jamal, like most of my students, was so far behind academically that he would never catch up during the traditional school day. The hours of 7:45 a.m. through 2:50 p.m. simply wouldn't suffice for Jamal. He needed something extra to give him the time to learn his multiplication and division facts (and a host of other academic skills he'd never mastered). I asked Jamal's family if he could stay for tutoring after school twice a week.

They readily agreed, and I was able to have some one-on-one instruction with Jamal. He quickly mastered the basic math that was a prerequisite for the higher-level math.

Jamal wasn't the only student who needed additional instructional time. I began tutoring students before school, after school, during lunch, and throughout recess. We created a class "scholar schedule," and students signed up for extra help. I eventually recruited other tutors to keep up with demand and ensure students received individual attention.

Spending time with four or five students in small groups also helped me develop better relationships with them and their families. We talked about everything from the latest episode of *Beverly Hills, 90210* to the upcoming Boyz II Men album. Students let me into their lives in such a natural and authentic way—by sharing hysterical reenactments of what happened over the weekend or describing where they hoped to be in ten years. Our class system of rewards grew to include a slot for two students to eat lunch with me in the classroom instead of joining their friends in the school cafeteria. What began as a response to a student's academic deficiencies evolved into a distinct and positive dynamic of our classroom community and culture.

Objectives Instead of Activities

As a first-year teacher, I had so much to learn. At times it seemed as if the lessons simply wouldn't stop coming my way. One of the most significant and humbling challenges—or refiner's fire—was set ablaze right before winter break. We had spent a few weeks on an oceanography unit. Students learned about ocean tides, sea life, and water conservation. The unit culminated in a two-day science lab during which we planned to dissect squids! I purchased fourteen small squids from a local seafood mart and brought them to our classroom.

The students, working in pairs, used tiny scalpels to cut open the sea creatures and identify their internal organs. My fifth-graders examined the animal's ink sack and tested the black liquid's consistency. We even found a recipe to make calamari after the dissection (only three brave souls were willing to taste it).

I was thrilled that my Teach For America mentor was observing my classroom that afternoon. Gloria was a veteran educator with over thirty years as a Compton teacher, administrator, and mentor. She definitely stood out when visiting Compton's public schools—an elderly Jewish woman with an East Coast fashion sense, who, despite having lived several decades on the West Coast, still had traces of her New York accent. But Gloria was the real deal. She knew the ins and outs of teaching at a deep level. Receiving her praise was extraordinary for any educator, but her critiques could be crushing. Given the stakes, I was thrilled Gloria was coming to visit me during the squid dissection. It was perfect timing!

After the squids had been safely disposed of and the students had been dismissed for recess, Gloria and I sat down to talk. She pulled out her notebook where she'd been recording thoughts and observations during the lesson.

"The students were having so much fun, Nicole," began Gloria. "Congratulations on finding a way to get them engaged at such a deep level."

I beamed.

"But I'm curious. Why were the students dissecting squids?"

"Well," I started, "it was the last part of our oceanography unit. I thought it would be a fun way to end the unit. The kids had never dissected anything before, and they were really excited about it!"

"That's fine," Gloria declared. "But why squids? And why did you dissect them?"

I must have looked puzzled, because she followed up with a few additional questions. "Did it connect to a broader study of squids? Had the students focused on invertebrates or mollusks during the unit so that dissecting squids was a natural connection point for them?"

"Um . . . well . . . not really," I stammered, feeling my face starting to flush.

Gloria's tone softened, as she realized I felt a bit exposed and unsure of what, if anything, my students actually learned that day. "Nicole, part of closing the achievement gap involves building strong relationships with your students, so you can motivate them to learn. Clearly you've done that, and you've built an environment of respect, community, and intellectual curiosity. But the other piece involves knowing what your students are learning and why they're learning it.

"You have to know how every single lesson connects to the broader goals you want to accomplish by the end of the lesson, the end of the unit, and the end of the school year," continued Gloria. "Otherwise, your students will continue to have fun, which is important, but they're less likely to master crucial skills; nor will they fully maximize their learning potential. You are doing some wonderful things here, and I want to make sure you and your class get to the next level."

I took a deep breath, attempting to absorb all she had said. She'd rightfully identified a missing piece of my efforts. By this time, we had accomplished some significant foundational elements: we had a healthy classroom culture; students demonstrated respect for me and for one another; families supported our academic goals; we'd found a way for students to get more classroom time in order to alleviate skill gaps. But Gloria was completely right. I had yet to ensure that with every lesson my students accomplished the most important thing: learning. Oh, sure, learning was happening—but we weren't making progress quickly enough.

During the winter holiday break, in addition to catching up on some much-needed sleep, I adjusted my classroom approach once again. I made sure each lesson had a clear learning objective connecting to our broader unit and year-end classroom goals. Fun activities were still a part of what we did, but I did my best to make sure it was *fun with a purpose.*

Planning lessons with an end goal in mind proved to be significantly more challenging. It was like completing a complex maze or logic puzzle—backward. But the results became apparent almost immediately. I made sure my class knew what they were learning and why they were learning it. Students not only understood why a particular lesson mattered; they also saw their own progress toward our larger academic goals. As a goal-oriented person myself, I should have realized sooner that my students would like the idea of seeing clear progress on concrete and meaningful goals. They became motivated in a way that I'd never expected! Thanks to Gloria, I took another crucial step toward closing the achievement gap that year.

The Evidence

My students took California's standardized test in late April. For better or worse, my school placed a huge emphasis on how our students performed on these comprehensive exams. While we didn't have the pressure to "teach to the test," which many teachers have since the federal government implemented No Child Left Behind in 2001,[2] I was fully aware that these tests were a weighty evaluation tool used to assign success or failure to a school, to my teaching abilities, and to my students' academic abilities. The test didn't fully measure everything my students learned that year (since we covered material far beyond the scope of one assessment). However, the test's objectives did link to the standardized test my students took in fourth grade, so it was a helpful way to measure what they learned between fourth and fifth grades. Also, because I knew it mattered for my students, it mattered to me.

When the results of the test were given to me, I discovered that my fifth graders, on average, had made about *two and a half years* of progress in math and about *one and a half years* in reading—in just one school year! Kids who couldn't read at the beginning of the year were reading introductory chapter books by the end. Students who couldn't do basic two-digit addition in September mastered complex fractions by June.

But something made an even deeper impact on me. More than one student actually confessed to me that they had never felt smart before, until that year in our classroom. I realize now that I was greatly blessed to witness lives that were literally being transformed before my eyes.

One of the most important lessons I learned teaching fifth grade in Compton is that the academic achievement gap doesn't have to exist. We *can* educate all children—even those from the poorest families—at very high levels. But, like most things that are worthwhile, it doesn't come easily.

Unable to celebrate for long, I had a moment of panic. What would happen when my kids went to middle school and high school? What if they got lost in a high school with two thousand other students and fell through the cracks? How can our school system ensure that kids continue to make significant academic progress annually? I have to admit, these questions have remained with me for years and have continually motivated my work on educational equity for the last two decades. I'm acutely aware that, while one year's worth of progress is fantastically inspiring, we need sustained transformational change. We need to multiply success stories at a higher and more systemic level than just one teacher's classroom.

Redefining Success

Fortunately, there are hundreds of successful examples that can inspire us and remind us that educational inequity can be solved. The KIPP (Knowledge Is Power Program) Academies are a shining example of what kids from the most challenging backgrounds can achieve. These public charter schools, now serving 20,000 students, were founded in 1995 by Dave Levin and Mike Feinberg and include eighty-two schools in nineteen states and the District of Columbia. Levin and Feinberg both taught in poor, urban neighborhoods in Houston and were aware of the challenges their students faced. But they also had a firm, unwavering belief in their students' limitless potential. They believed that through hard work, extended time in the classroom, and extremely high expectations, all students could achieve.

Eighty percent of KIPP students are from low-income families, and 90 percent are African American or Latino. Children who start in KIPP Academies at the fourth grade score very low on state tests: 41 percent in math and 31 percent in reading. But after four years in a KIPP school, these same students do remarkably better on eighth-grade tests: 80 percent in math and 58 percent in reading. And in communities where only one out of every student graduates from college, more than 80 percent of KIPP alumni have gone on to college. These results are simply phenomenal. Clearly, these students are significantly beating the odds and surpassing the academic performance of other kids in their communities. The KIPP Academies are literally changing the life prospects for the children they serve.[3]

Another example of a school system that effectively educates low-income students is IDEA Public Schools in rural south Texas, with sixteen schools, some of them in the third-poorest county in the United States—where only one out of every twenty adults has a college degree. This school district has destroyed the myth that poor and minority students cannot achieve. Since the first class of IDEA high school seniors graduated in 2007, 100 percent of their graduating seniors have been accepted to a four-year college or university.[4] The National Center for Educational Achievement listed the school district (as well as five individual schools within the district) as "exemplary"—their highest rating, which is based on standardized tests.[5]

Another school district in Texas that is making the news is YES Prep, a charter school system in Houston, with six middle schools and four high schools serving 5,400 students, most of them low-income students. In 2012, two of YES Prep's high schools were given gold medal rankings by *US News & World Report*, which measures college readiness and proficiency in math and reading.[6] And the school system recently won a national award given to the best public charter school, for its record of outstanding academic progress.[7]

Some traditional public schools and neighborhood schools also demonstrate tremendous student achievement results. One such school, Baylor-Woodson Elementary School, in Inkster, Michigan, has a student population of more than 80 percent poor families—many of whom face severe economic challenges and even homelessness. The school resides in a poor, urban area near Detroit and the student body is predominantly African American.

But demographics do not determine the outcomes for kids at Baylor-Woodson. In 2011 the school received a prestigious Dispelling the Myth Award by Education Trust, a national nonprofit and advocacy organization. And here's why: 73 percent of the school's fifth-graders scored as advanced in math in 2010, compared with 45 percent in the state. In reading, 63 percent scored as advanced, compared with 44 percent statewide. Parents and teachers describe a laser-like focus on student achievement, high-quality instruction, and outstanding professional development options for teachers as keys to their success.[8]

So, yes, there is good news! As my teaching experience demonstrates, we certainly need to put in a lot of hard work to see results. But we *can* see results. And if we can see significant results in hundreds and thousands of classrooms and schools (and even, increasingly, at the school district level), it's undeniable that this type of success can be replicated. Just as the Bible tells Christians to proclaim the good news of the gospel, I believe that we must declare the good news of low-income public schools. Success is possible! Let's not keep the news to ourselves. As the familiar Christian camp song admonishes us, "Shout it from the mountaintop . . . I want the world to know."[9] I guarantee that everyone, those who live in low-income communities and those who live in more privileged communities, are desperate to hear a bit of good news about public schools.

4

A Rich History, an Absent Voice

In my view there is a sense in which education ought
to be democratic and another sense in which it ought
not. It ought to be democratic in the sense of being
available, without distinction of sex, colour, class,
race, or religion, to all who can—and will—dili-
gently accept it. But once the young people are inside
the school there must be no attempt to establish
a factitious egalitarianism between the idlers and
dunces on the one hand and the clever and indus-
trious on the other. A modern nation needs a very
large class of genuinely educated people and it is
the primary function of schools and universities
to supply them. To lower standards or disguise inequalities is fatal.

—C. S. Lewis[1]

I am always energized when I meet other Christians who share
my enthusiasm for improving urban public schools. We have

created an informal network. I reach out regularly to my faith-based public school reformers for encouragement, prayer, and advice; sometimes we simply need to commiserate and share good old-fashioned rants. This work has lots of ups and downs, and we definitely need to support one another.

Often our conversations yield more than I anticipate, and my meeting with Jeremy proved to be one of those occasions. Jeremy, a young minister and nonprofit leader in New York City, runs an organization that helps churches build partnerships with public schools. Jeremy has been at this work for quite some time and has a true passion and relentless energy for turning around failing public schools.

During a trip to New York City, I invited Jeremy to join me for coffee to share updates on our respective work. Eager to talk with my brother in this movement, I grabbed a table at one of the many Starbucks in midtown Manhattan, and we launched into our conversation. I'd been building relationships with faith-based organizations, hoping to inspire them to help close the academic achievement gap, but I ran into some stumbling blocks. I was curious to hear Jeremy's perspective on which was more challenging: inspiring Christians to partner with public schools or convincing public school principals to open their doors to people of faith who want to help them.

"That's a tough question," he replied. "I suppose there's a degree of reluctance on both sides. But I think Christians have a way to go if we want to prove our relevance to urban communities. Many schools don't think we have anything to offer." I was somewhat surprised by this characterization, given the important role that many faith communities have in African American and Latino/Hispanic neighborhoods. Churches are often the center of urban communities and a place of civic and spiritual engagement. So I encouraged him to elaborate.

Jeremy went on to describe a conversation he had with a friend who is an elementary school principal in the Bronx. His friend taught for several years, then moved into school administration over a decade ago. Jeremy reached out to him to gauge his interest in possible church-school partnerships.

"He asked me if he could be honest with me, and of course I told him yes," Jeremy began slowly. "Then he told me something I'll probably never forget: 'In my twenty years of working in the Bronx, the neighborhood churches have only reached out to me two times. One time they came to lobby for prayer in public schools. The other time they protested a new science curriculum that included evolution. Twice they contact me in twenty years—and they wanted to talk about school prayer and evolution. But you know what? For twenty years I've had kids that cannot read or do basic math. My students struggle to make it through school. We don't have enough books, supplies, or resources for them. Our school building is literally crumbling around us. The kids have life-threatening, urgent needs. They're hungry; they're homeless. But in all these years, you've only criticized. You've never helped. Taking evolution out of my textbooks won't change a thing for my kids. They'll still be poor, uneducated, and stuck in the cycle of poverty. But not one church person has ever asked me about any of those things.'"

Jeremy took a long pause and continued. "My friend said he wouldn't welcome the church in his school because, as far as he could see, they couldn't care less about what kids in poverty really need to succeed in school."

I wish with all my heart that Jeremy's friend were an outlier. I would love to think this story is a mere aberration. Surely churches throughout America have rallied to support students in poor communities. After all, churches have the people, money, resources, social capital, and political capital that can potentially help turn the tide for millions of public school children. Surely we wouldn't turn our backs on a problem with clear biblical and theological underpinnings?

However, it seems Christians, on the whole, have abandoned a deep commitment to public schools. By that I don't suggest that all Christians have ceased to send their own children to public schools. That may be the case for some Christians who choose religious schools or homeschooling, but I assess our commitment to public schools somewhat differently. The crucial question we need to ask is: to what extent is the Christian community working to help improve public schools for poor children—regardless of where we choose to send our own children?

While many White evangelical Christians may have avoided public schools altogether, other Christians—including Catholics, African Americans, Hispanics, and many Protestants—have been actively engaged in the work of quality education for poor and minority children for decades. Although some African Americans and Latinos have acquired the resources to move to wealthier suburbs, the problem of educational inequity has been nearly impossible for Christians of color to avoid because it disproportionately impacts their ethnic communities. While the work of African American and Latino Christians is extremely important and meaningful, God has not given this mandate only to Christians of color.

The New Evangelical and Public Schools

"Some Christians vote on other values, thank you very much," I declared to our television set on a November night in 2004. The presidential election returns poured in, and President George W. Bush had just won reelection. At that moment I was less concerned with whom our country elected than I was with the way the media conducted its election postmortem. Nearly every pundit credited the evangelical Christian voters as a significant voting bloc that tipped the race for Republicans. According to the analysts, Evangelicals were completely swayed by the values debate around abortion and gay marriage. Really? All Evangelicals are two-issue voters? This assertion felt completely inconsistent with my own reality.

After my husband calmed me down, I was still struck by the difference between how the media presented Evangelicals and how my friends and I voted as Evangelicals. I could not find a single media story about evangelical Christians whose values compelled them to vote for the candidate with the best platform to eliminate poverty, bring equity to the disenfranchised, or live out what Isaiah 1:17 admonishes: "Learn to do right; seek justice. Defend the oppressed." I knew we existed. After all, that was me and most of my friends! How did our perspectives become nonexistent? Where was our voice? How did this overpowering political narrative influence the degree to which Christians believe other social issues require our attention?

Several years later I'm happy to report that the narrative has begun to shift. During the last few years, evangelical Christians, historically portrayed as less engaged in social justice issues, have taken up causes such as creation care and man-made climate change, global poverty, HIV/AIDS, and comprehensive immigration reform. National evangelical organizations advocate increasing United States foreign assistance to sub-Saharan Africa and push the federal government to relieve debt from developing countries. The "new Evangelical" has committed to demonstrate Christ's love through justice-wielding actions. Thanks to organizations like Faith in Public Life—a strategy center to help raise the voices of progressive people of faith (I served on the board from 2010 to 2012)—these actions are garnering attention in mainstream media. Dozens of media stories and articles have highlighted this trend, including articles in *Time* magazine, the *New Yorker* magazine, the *Washington Post*, and the *New York Times*.[2]

But on the whole, the Christian community has not prioritized public education reform. The time is ripe for Christians to engage in one of the last frontiers of justice in our nation: ensuring that children in low-income communities receive the education they deserve. We can no longer stand on the sidelines. If we do, we risk becoming irrelevant to thousands of principals like Jeremy's friend. We will miss the opportunity to help empower millions of American children with a quality education.

As we build a case for engaging in public schools beyond the causes that Jeremy's friend describes, it is important to understand the context and history through which Christians come to public education reform. How did we get to the point where we have minimal (at best) involvement with public schools? What holds us back from delving into an issue that seems tailor-made for people of faith?

I explore these themes not to condemn the Christian community. Rather, I bring our past to bear in the hope that we can better understand and acknowledge it. If necessary, we may need to repent in order to move forward and help children who desperately need us.

A Christian Tradition: Educating Poor Children

As much as I'd like to take credit for identifying a brand-new arena in which Christians can engage, faith communities actually have a rich history of working to educate children in low-income communities. Our near-absence from schools in poor neighborhoods is a relatively new phenomenon. We can take a quick journey to the United Kingdom and learn that devout Christian leaders championed this cause as early as the late eighteenth century. One of the most influential leaders of the time, William Wilberforce, is well known to many Christians and non-Christians alike. But Wilberforce's commitment to educate poor children remains relatively obscure.

My mom and dad both went to Wilberforce University, a historically Black college in southwestern Ohio. I grew up hearing about their beloved Wilberforce, how they fell in love and became college sweethearts on campus. Like most parents who have a fondness for their alma mater, they forced me and my brother to endure more than one family trip to the campus during our childhood. Mom and Dad regaled us with stories about favorite hangouts, roommate shenanigans, and how they managed to stitch together fun as Black young adults in 1960s rural Ohio (three words: get a car).

Hearing these stories throughout my youth, I didn't make the connection between their small college and the famous British abolitionist William Wilberforce. I saw the 2006 film *Amazing Grace*, based on Eric Metaxas's gripping book *Amazing Grace: William Wilberforce and the Heroic Campaign to End Slavery*.[3] I began to reflect on the connections between his amazing life story and my parents' tiny college campus in rural Ohio.

As I read more about Wilberforce's life, I was surprised to learn about his passion concerning a host of other social ills—including education reform. Wilberforce was a part of the Clapham Sect, a group of wealthy and influential evangelical Christians who committed their lives to improving conditions for England's poor and disenfranchised.[4] The philanthropists, politicians, authors, and clergy who made up the group deeply believed that Christianity compelled its followers to make the world a better place. These core beliefs fueled Wilberforce's faith-motivated campaign to ensure children in urban slums learned to read and write.

William Wilberforce and Hannah More, another Clapham member, began discussing how to improve nearby Cheddar, a community of people living in abject poverty. The residents lived in extremely challenging circumstances; most dwelled in hovels or caves. Wilberforce spent some time in the nearby village and resolved to take action to improve the living conditions and circumstances. The community was essentially illiterate, so the Clapham Sect decided to start a school. Over the next ten years Hannah More opened more than a dozen "Sunday schools" in Cheddar.[5] Where others overlooked these forgotten people, Wilberforce and More saw potential. Their Christian convictions propelled them to educate men, women, and children in Cheddar.

Wilberforce University was founded in 1856, thousands of miles from Cheddar, England. As my parents often remind me, it is the oldest private, historically Black college in the United States. How fitting that their college, which was founded to educate a racial group that many previously thought to be uneducable, was named after a man who educated thousands of poor and disenfranchised people of England.

The Clapham leaders weren't the only trailblazing British Christians who championed education for poor children. Sunday school, as we know it today, began with a very different purpose. Prominent Christian leaders who originally established Sunday schools made a direct connection between Sunday teachings and closing the (yet-to-be-named) academic achievement gap.

Like many children reared in churchgoing families, I attended Sunday school classes during much of my childhood. I recall being led downstairs to our church basement before the main church service began. Dozens of perfectly coiffed girls sashayed around in taffeta dresses with black patent leather shoes; the boys sported miniature suits with the requisite clip-on ties. My parents deposited us to volunteer teachers who divided us into age-appropriate groups.

We sat in classrooms with small, metal chairs while my Sunday school teachers taught us to sing catchy, Christian kid favorites like "Jesus Loves Me" and "The B-I-B-L-E." Our teachers focused on Bible stories that were adventurous and dramatic enough to hold our short attention spans: Noah and the great flood, Daniel in the lion's den, and Jonah in the belly of the whale. The very nature of their instructional techniques assumed we were literate by a certain age; they had students read Bible verses aloud. As far as I can recall, the teachers focused on my spiritual development and not my academic progress.

Years later I was astonished to learn that the modern-day Sunday school movement has its roots in a Christian-motivated desire to educate children in poor communities. Robert Raikes, a philanthropist and devout Anglican who lived in England during the eighteenth century, led this charge. Raikes's father owned the local newspaper and turned the management over to Robert. The *Gloucester Journal* became Robert's platform for social justice. First he turned his attention to England's horrid prison system. Prisoners lived in rancid conditions and did not receive enough food. Those who didn't have families who could afford to bring them more food had to beg other prisoners to share their meals. In short, it was a demeaning and deplorable way of life.[6]

Raikes exposed the prison system and brought awareness to a major social ill. His writings inspired wealthy citizens to donate food and clothing to struggling prisoners. But he also realized something greater. He decided the most strategic way to eliminate problems in England's prison system was to reduce the number of men who ended up there. What was the best way to do that? Raikes determined that children needed a quality education so they could have better options in life.[7] (Times haven't changed much, huh?)

Free public education did not exist yet in England. Wealthy families could afford private tutors and governesses for young children. When the boys from these families got older, they usually attended boarding schools (girls stayed at home and, in some cases, continued their private tutoring instruction). The vast majority of children during Raikes's time did not have access to schools, nor was it a priority to educate the working class and poor. When these children weren't working on their parents' farms or performing household duties, many of them would run freely about the streets—particularly on Sundays, when the children had no work responsibilities.

I can imagine Raikes wandering through the impoverished slums, watching children roaming around and getting into mischief, as children will do. Perhaps their tattered clothes or gaunt faces caught his attention. Maybe he asked a ten-year-old boy to read the sign over a village shop and the little guy couldn't do it. Or possibly the contrast between his childhood and that of these youngsters opened his eyes to disparities he'd never realized. We may never know the specifics, but something pricked Raikes's heart on a particular trip through town. He worried that many of these children would wind up in the impoverished jails he'd been writing about. Christ-centered mercy and compassion provoked him to support these children, in the hope that they would become literate and have a greater chance at life's opportunities.

Other philanthropists of Raikes's era considered creating free schools for poor children that would provide instruction Monday through Friday. When that was deemed too expensive, they joined with Raikes to create a school every Sunday (one day of instruction was better than none, they seemed to reason). Raikes and his Sunday school teachers used the Bible as the main literacy text. The schools flourished, and within seven years more than 250,000 children attended Sunday schools—many of them learning to read for the first time in their lives.[8] The Sunday school movement caught on in America. Christian leaders like D. L. Moody educated thousands of children through Sunday schools in urban Chicago.[9]

William Wilberforce, Hannah More, Robert Raikes, D. L. Moody, and many other giants in Christian history caught on to something that many of us seem to have missed. I am so grateful these leaders recognized a unique synergy between their Christian beliefs and the need to educate children in poor neighborhoods. When we look back on some of the language these leaders used to describe undereducated populations, we might cringe at their patronizing terms (compared to our respectful and inclusive modern-day terminology). A more cynical eye may even cast aspersions on their motives. Did they look down on these children? Did early Christian leaders see them as a group of unwanted children to "save"? Should they have gone further to seek the type of transformational and holistic change those families likely needed? Perhaps.

But it's also true that they saw all children as worthy and deserving of education, care, and respect. Wilberforce, More, and Raikes helped create a new reality for hundreds of thousands of children. Let us look to them as faithful examples whose Christian principles propelled them to improve education for the most disenfranchised children.

Protestant Influence on Early American Public Schools

"Don't we want to keep the separation of church and state?" asked one of my fellow attendees at an education policy forum. A rigorous panel discussion about school funding and equity had just ended, and I stayed after the event to mingle and do the obligatory chitchat and business-card exchange. While sharing verbal pleasantries, I told her the quick version of what I do. It seemed to strike a chord with her, albeit a negative one.

"I cannot imagine why we'd want to encourage religious people to get involved with public schools," she said. "After all, we've gotten along just fine these past two hundred years without Christians in schools. I worry that Christians would simply muddy the waters and overly complicate our already sensitive education reform efforts."

After informing my new friend that I shared her deep belief in the importance of a healthy church–state separation, I launched into a two-minute history lesson. I politely pushed back on her assumption that Christians and other religious people haven't played a role in the history of American public education.

Given the minimal involvement of Christians in public school reform today, it's easy to believe that Christians have largely been absent from US public school development or reform. But in reality, this is inaccurate. Christians are simply unengaged *now*. Ironically, public education in the United States has deep roots in the Protestant religious tradition. This historical influence was not without its share of hypocrisy (and would certainly present significant problems for contemporary church–state separation). But it is worth noting this history, as it sets up a striking contrast to the extent that many Christians have retreated from a system that they literally helped create.

America's original thirteen colonies operated "town schools" in each local community; local towns and villages had the sole responsibility to educate children within their jurisdictions. Given their resources and structure, most towns facilitated their local schools through the church, so schools had religious imprints throughout the system. The Puritans sponsored schools in most New England colonies. Quakers and other religious denominations led the Mid-Atlantic colonies' schools.[10]

Not surprisingly, biblical and religious teachings were at the core of what students learned. *The New England Primer*, the central student textbook for several decades, was explicitly Christian. Children learned to read, in part, by mastering Bible stories and verses. These religious groups viewed educating children and ensuring basic literacy skills as a part of their faith-based mandate.

While it's important to note that girls, minorities, and poor families generally got shortchanged at these schools (if they were allowed to attend at all), it is impossible to overlook the central role Christians played in starting free public schools. Christians considered it their duty and responsibility to educate children in their communities.

In the next section we'll turn our attention to how Lutherans and Catholics provide parochial education in low-income communities. While neither denomination focuses on public education, they are one step closer than many contemporary Christian groups in helping to close the achievement gap by emphasizing educating children in poor, urban neighborhoods.

Urban Lutheran Schools

Two Christian groups in the United States have a history of educating low-income urban students. During the last several decades, Lutheran and Catholic schools have responded to the needs of urban children by providing alternatives to inner-city public schools. While neither group has done so willingly (they were both victims of radical demographic shifts in the latter part of the twentieth century), their commitment to urban populations is worth exploring. How does each of these denominations understand its responsibility to educate poor and minority children, and what can other Christians learn from their example?

Lutheran schools sprang up in the United States before compulsory public education. German and Scandinavian Lutherans immigrated to America and immediately founded their own schools as early as the middle of the eighteenth century. The Lutheran Church–Missouri Synod (LCMS), the second-largest Lutheran denomination in the United States, exemplifies the religion's strong educational tradition that was handed down from Martin Luther. As of 2012, LCMS operates more than three thousand early childhood and elementary schools across the nation.[11]

As I mentioned in an earlier chapter, my brother and I attended a Lutheran elementary school in Detroit. Greenfield Peace, while not the most prestigious or competitive private school, was a better alternative to the public schools in our neighborhood. While some school families were affiliated with the church, which sat across the street from the school, many families, like mine, were not. According to my mother, most families simply wanted to give their children a better education than that offered at their local public schools.

We definitely got schooled in the ways of religion (much to our chagrin, at times). We attended weekly chapel services, memorized Bible verses, and learned a host of folk-inspired Christian songs of that era. Yet the overall school culture had a heavy focus on academics and character building. I never remember any religious agenda being forced on me. When several of my friends went through Lutheran confirmation classes in seventh and eighth grades, I felt no pressure to join this tradition. It was completely acceptable to be a non-Lutheran at Greenfield Peace.

When White residents rapidly fled Detroit during the 1970s and 1980s, African Americans became the overwhelming majority in our Lutheran school. My kindergarten class picture from 1974 included eight White students. By the time I graduated from eighth grade in 1983, there was just one white student in our entire class of about thirty children.

The students' economic background changed during my nine years at Greenfield Peace. The school became decidedly more working class. The teachers began to wrestle with some of the difficult challenges that befall many schools in urban areas. The administrators and teachers, who all were White, continued to press forward. While many private schools in Detroit closed during the 1970s and 1980s, my school remained a high-quality, affordable alternative for many urban families. The faculty and administration demonstrated a commitment to our academic success.

Jane Buerger, an education professor and dean with the Lutheran-based Concordia University System, noted this demographic shift as a broader trend with urban Lutheran schools.

> As the pool of school-age Lutheran children decreased, neighborhoods, especially urban ones, often underwent a population shift. As black and Latino residents moved in, the white community left. Those who stayed with the Lutheran church were generally those whose children were grown. Schools that were able to adapt to the changing neighborhood have, in some cases, thrived.[12]

One could justifiably argue that Lutheran urban schools have developed by default due to circumstantial demographic shifts, as opposed to a broader church mandate to serve the poor. But to its credit, the Lutheran Church–Missouri Synod has engaged proactively to support the changing face of urban Lutheran schools. They have created a system and structure for urban Lutheran schools to network and share resources. LCMS also created a scholarship program to ensure that urban and minority students can continue to afford Lutheran schools. Most important, at a time when many White institutions abandoned urban cities, the Lutheran schools didn't close their doors to kids like me and my brother.

Urban Catholic Schools

In 2011, Teach For America held its 20th Anniversary Summit. The national nonprofit organization hosted several thousand alumni who completed the two-year teaching requirement during the last two decades. The gathering featured prominent speakers and educators, such as United States congressman and civil rights icon John Lewis, United States education secretary Arne Duncan, and *The Tipping Point* author Malcolm Gladwell.

This summit included dozens of breakout sessions where participants could explore specific topics. I had the privilege of planning a breakout session about how people of faith can help close the academic achievement gap. Several national faith leaders, of all religious backgrounds, graciously joined our panel, including Teach For America alumna Stephanie Saroki de Garcia. Stephanie cofounded Seton Education Partners, an organization that supports urban Catholic education.[13]

Most of the panelists were twenty years Stephanie's senior, but she held her own throughout the lively discussion. She kept reminding us of the specific Catholic mandate to improve opportunities for low-income children. At one point Stephanie declared, "This is what Catholics do. We help the poor and disenfranchised. So, of course, improving academic opportunities for children in our poorest neighborhoods is what we should do. It's deeply Catholic." The audience broke into spontaneous applause. What lessons can the rest of the Christian community learn from the Catholic Church's focus on urban education?

Prior to 1925 the United States didn't allow Catholic schools to have an official presence. But the Supreme Court decision *Pierce v. Society of Sisters* declared state laws requiring students to attend public schools to be unconstitutional. After that the Catholic Church built schools at a remarkable rate. In 1875 there were fewer than 1,500 Catholic schools in America; by 1930 that number had increased to more than 10,000.[14] The massive postwar baby boom produced nearly 80 million American children. Between 1941 and 1960, non-public-school enrollment, driven by Catholic schools, grew by 117 percent. When it reached its apex in the mid-1960s, the nation's Catholic K–12 education system maintained more than 13,000 schools, serving more than 5 million children—approximately 12 percent of all American students. Most of these schools were in cities, such as Boston, Chicago, Detroit, and Pittsburgh.[15]

But in the 1950s and 1960s, many Catholic families moved to the suburbs, thanks to a prosperous postwar economy. Most suburban Catholic families opted to send their children to high-quality suburban public schools; therefore, Catholic school enrollment began to decline, particularly in urban communities. Catholic schools traditionally kept costs low by employing nuns, priests, friars, and other clergy who didn't require salaries. But their labor force quickly shifted to Catholic laypeople. This new generation of Catholic teachers demanded higher salaries and benefits more in line with those of their public school counterparts. Older facilities began to decay and required expensive repairs. The confluence of these factors caused thousands of Catholic schools to shut their doors. By the beginning of the twenty-first century, the number of Catholic schools had dropped to 5,300.[16]

It would have been easy for the Catholic Church to turn its back on urban Catholic schools; many urban families didn't have the financial resources to pay tuition or support the school financially. While many Catholic schools in urban centers have had no choice but to close, there is a fever within the American Catholic Church to save these schools. Why? Three words: Catholic social teaching.

Catholic social teaching began as early as the late 1800s and has been refined by several popes and Catholic leaders. The United States Conference of Catholic Bishops adopted several general principles that help American Catholics understand how to live in a just and compassionate manner commensurate with biblical teachings. These seven principles range from topics as diverse as "Life and Dignity of the Human Person" to "Care for God's Creation." The principle that speaks to urban education is "Option for the Poor and Vulnerable," which states,

> A basic moral test is how our most vulnerable members are faring. In a society marred by deepening divisions between rich and poor, our tradition recalls the story of the Last Judgment (Matt. 25:31–46) and instructs us to put the needs of the poor and vulnerable first.[17]

This notion of how we treat "the poor and vulnerable" underscores the importance of urban education and closing the achievement gap. Catholic leaders view urban Catholic schools as a key strategy by which they can fulfill Catholic social teaching doctrines. As one prominent Catholic scholar stated, "The implications for Catholic schools are obvious. If segments of the population are marginalized, the Church is obliged to make extraordinary efforts to rectify social fragmentation."[18] Several documents take this idea a step further by critiquing Catholic schools that continue to educate solely the elite.

> Since education is an important means of improving the social and economic condition of the individual and of peoples, if the Catholic school were to turn its attention exclusively or predominantly to those from the wealthier social classes, it could be contributing towards maintaining their privileged position, and could thereby continue to favor a society which is unjust.[19]

What Holds Us Back?

Christians have a deep historical involvement with urban education, from eighteenth-century England, colonial America, and the steadfast work of Lutheran and Catholic urban schools during the last forty years. Given that rich history, why are so many twenty-first-century Christians working on social justice causes but not yet comprehensively working to improve public education for low-income children?

Desegregation and the Unfortunate Rise of Christian Schools

This topic isn't fun or easy to talk about—but we need to. Christians are not without fault in race relations. We have a complex history with respect to racial issues in the United States, and unfortunately that history can influence how we choose to engage with children who are affected by the academic achievement gap.

As noted in an earlier chapter, America has a less-than-stellar track record of providing quality education to children of color and to recent immigrants. African Americans were not allowed to attend schools during the time of slavery, and in some states it was against the law to teach a slave to read. Even after our nation outlawed slavery, the 1896 United States Supreme Court decision *Plessy v. Ferguson* declared that Blacks and Whites could maintain separate school facilities (and pretty much everything else) as long as the entities were "separate but equal."

But the civil rights movement of the 1950s and 1960s brought radical changes to this dysfunctional and inherently unequal system. After years of legal maneuvers, most Americans, of all races and backgrounds, celebrated when the United States Supreme Court ruled to end school segregation, in the landmark 1954 ruling *Brown v. Board of Education*.

I'd like to think that all of my Christian brothers and sisters were on the side of integration, simply because African American children would now have (at least in theory) the same educational opportunities that had been afforded to White children. After all, if God created every child and endowed each with "certain unalienable rights," shouldn't devout Christians rejoice when systemic injustice is brought to its knees?

But a funny thing happened when public schools were forced to admit African American children alongside White students. The number of Christian schools grew. This phenomenon was particularly rampant in the South, where desegregation met some of its strongest resistance. Some scholars go so far as to assert that Christians created private schools in direct response to mandatory desegregation. David Nevin and Robert E. Bills conducted a 1976 study, *The Schools That Fear Built*, which labeled many Christian schools "white flight academies."[20] Their study was among the first to bring attention to the independent Christian schools that developed in the desegregated South. Nevin and Bills argued that these institutions originated to accommodate White parents who did not want to send their children to racially integrated schools.

While these assertions seem almost unconscionable in the twenty-first century, the church—particularly some of the more fundamentalist and evangelical segments—carries this legacy. I certainly cannot look into any person's heart to determine his or her motives for sending a child to a Christian school. Clearly, not every parent who made that choice in the 1960s (or who makes that decision today) is doing it for racist reasons. That said, for some Christian communities the opportunity to send children to an all-White Christian academy certainly did abdicate responsibility for improving conditions for children left behind in integrated public schools—particularly when some of those same parents likely had open disdain for or fear of the children now attending that school. What's the motivation to want to help ensure those children receive a quality education?

How does this sad and shameful part of our history impact the Christian community's involvement in public education today? While I cannot prove a direct correlation, I assert that this legacy, at the very least, may have hindered some Christians from feeling connected, responsible, or accountable for low-income public schools. Conversely, some public school communities whose families still recall the residual sting of segregated Christian academies may be less welcoming when Christians approach their schools to volunteer or help in some way. We should ask ourselves some pointed questions. In what ways is the Christian community fully seeking racial reconciliation for these previous wrongs? Have we fully acknowledged our collective history in response to racial integration? Until we discuss this openly and honestly, it will likely hinder our efforts to become a force for public school equity.

Christian Counterculture

The late 1950s and early 1960s brought radical changes to American culture. The separation between church and state became more defined, especially with the United States Supreme Court's 1962 decision *Engel v. Vitale*, banning prayer in public schools.[21] Greater secularization sparked more evangelical and fundamentalist Christians to start their own schools. Many parents sought to separate their children from what they perceived as anti-Christian beliefs and ideologies.[22]

Some Christians continue to retreat from public schools, in part because they want to educate their children with a distinct Christian worldview and protect them from a wide range of diverse ideologies and ideas. Homeschooling is an option that many parents, regardless of religious or nonreligious background, choose for a variety of reasons, but statistics show that Christians choose this option at disproportionate rates. In 2007 the National Center for Education Statistics asked parents why they chose to homeschool; just over two-thirds of the parents cited religious and moral reasons.[23] How does this retreat from public schools impact some Christians' sense of responsibility for improving public education? Could there be unintended consequences?

I succumbed to the Facebook revolution a couple of years ago. Initially it provided a great way to connect with long-lost friends from junior high and share pictures of our children. But it also took me into a new world of fascinating and controversial virtual debates. One day I linked to a blog post I'd written about how Christians can get involved to improve educational outcomes in public schools. Most of my friends "liked" the post and said they found it interesting or thought-provoking (have I mentioned that I love my friends?), but one of my friends shared a different perspective.

"Why should Christians become involved in helping public schools?" she wrote. "After all, they've taken prayer out of schools and basically banned us from talking about God in any way, shape, or form. And now they want our help? The best thing we can do is fight to bring prayer back in schools!"

I was slightly stunned, particularly since I like to keep my Facebook world fairly benign and pleasant (which has made me rethink posting such things in the future). But never one to shy away from sharing my opinion, I did my best to respectfully express my perspective and encourage an overall sense of accountability to students in low-income public schools—even if we disagree with church–state separation. (I'm happy to report that the two of us are still friends. I've learned that disagreeing civilly can be tough but is definitely something worth striving for!)

This anecdote represents some of the lingering challenges the Christian community faces as we try to build a movement around public school inequity. Christians may feel less inclined to get involved with a system while there is a sense, among some Christians, that religion was unceremoniously booted from the premises. My friend's sentiment, whether we think it's right or wrong, represented her honest feelings. I personally believe this hurdle can be overcome, but we need to continually make the case that our involvement in public schools is about the children, regardless of what we think about the broader policies. If we reiterate the Christian mandate to care for all of God's children, particularly those affected by poverty, we can mobilize more people to work for much-needed justice.

Pragmatic Challenges

A few years ago I attended a faith-based justice conference. While none of the speakers focused on education, it was a wonderful opportunity to meet other people of faith who have a passion for equity and justice. I wanted to learn how other faith-based movements motivate and sustain interest in their particular cause.

I joined a session about the environment, or creation care, as the Christian leader defined it. She articulated a clear biblical case for why Christians should care about the environment and effectively steward the planet's resources. The session leader presented compelling evidence regarding the long-term dangers of not taking better care of the earth. What I loved the most were the clear "asks" she made of the audience. She asked each of us to do this one thing: go back to our homes and churches and switch every lightbulb to a more energy-efficient bulb. Conference staff actually handed us energy-efficient bulbs as we exited the session.

Brilliant, I thought. Solving our planet's complex environmental challenges will certainly require more than each of us switching our lightbulbs, but today, at the faith-based session, we were told to change our lightbulbs. And you know what? I went home and changed the lightbulbs in our house. This seemingly small action did not negate the massively complicated environmental issues with which we grapple, including our dependence on oil, our freshwater distribution system, and our need for sweeping federal legislation regarding the environment. But it did raise my awareness and helped me make a small difference.

Dozens of other causes have found "quick and easy" ways for constituents to take action. Our family sponsors a child with World Vision, an international child welfare and poverty relief organization. For a dollar a day (which is conveniently withdrawn from our checking account each month), we ensure that a little boy in Mozambique has a chance at a better life.

After watching a film by the National Humane Society, I immediately began making sure I purchased food from farms where animals are treated ethically. Each of these organizations, and many more like them, has found straightforward action items to support their issues.

What is the comparable you-can-go-home-and-do-this-now action to help improve low-income public schools? The education landscape is complex, to be certain, but those of us in the field have not created simple and compelling ways for individuals to get involved. I often worry that we make the problem seem overwhelming, which limits people of faith (and many others) from jumping in to help improve public schools. While no silver bullet exists, we will address several tangible ways to make an impact in later chapters.

Leadership Void, Race, and Apathy

We hear Christians speak out against a host of equity issues, but our community has a leadership void when it comes to public schools and the achievement gap. Where is the national outcry and outrage from faith leaders? Where are the prophetic voices rising up to demand that our country take the necessary steps to improve schools?

As I mentioned previously, in my travels around the country it's rare that a faith-based conference highlights educational inequity in the United States. And a quick stroll around any Christian bookstore will turn up dozens of faith-centered books about poverty, hunger, and global disease. But rarely, if at all, will the bookshelves contain any titles about American public schools (with the exception of books that critique American schools for removing prayer or promoting a secular, humanist agenda). In fact, it has become more likely to hear mainstream faith leaders speak about the lack of quality education for girls in developing countries than about the deplorable educational conditions for many poor children right here in our own country.

The exceptions, by and large, come from urban faith communities. People of color and people from low-income communities disproportionately feel the weight of the academic achievement gap. As a child growing up in the Black church, I can attest that the achievement gap was alive and well and living right outside the doors of our church. African American and Latino pastors and clergy are aware of the educational inequity, because it often impacts their congregation members. Many urban pastors speak about the achievement gap with some regularity. African American and Latino church leaders have even started parochial schools or public charter schools, in response to poor-quality public schools. These leaders are well aware of the need for other options. African American clergy, in particular, have championed vouchers (a highly debated policy that provides parents with a monetary "voucher" to send their child to any private or parochial school) in many cities around the nation.

While we need clergy of color and urban congregations to engage in the movement to eliminate public education inequity, their participation doesn't relieve the remaining Christian community from responsibility. Few Christian leaders have used their pulpits or media influence to shine a light on this issue, which likely plays a role in some Christians' apathy toward public education reform. Perhaps further adding to apathy, when we do hear about this issue within communities of faith it's often from people of color. We need advocates in every sector of the Christian community—regardless of our ethnic or economic background—otherwise, we run the risk of many of our brothers and sisters abdicating their responsibility. The achievement gap isn't an issue just for Christians in African American and Latino churches.

Given the urgent challenges in low-income public schools, it's futile and unproductive to spend energy blaming the evangelical Christian community for any of its prior actions. This is simply the reality of our history. Still, it is important to understand what may have inadvertently driven us to overlook public education inequity in this country. After decades of either disengagement from or battles with the public school, many Christians need a new mind-set to truly view improving public education as a biblical mandate. Even if we make the personal choice to send our own children to private or parochial schools, and even if the public schools do not conform to our specific values, we cannot continue to turn our backs on the millions of children growing up in poverty. We must find a way to work within the public education system and advocate for equal opportunity for all children. The remaining chapters detail a faith-based response to help improve low-income public schools.

5

A Biblical Framework

Children, Justice, and Human Potential

If Jesus were teaching in a public school today, I
think he'd choose to work here.
—A teacher in South Central Los Angeles

Although Christians' involvement with inner-city public schools
has been minimal in the last few decades, as we just explored,
there are biblical reasons why we should consider taking a
more proactive role. Recently, I spent several months deeply
engaged in conversations with Christian teachers and other
faith-motivated individuals who work with low-income public
schools who helped me gain a deeper understanding of biblical
themes that underlie their personal work. Each person's story
uniquely inspired and challenged me; their ideas resonated with
many of my core convictions. But Melanie, a fourth-year South
Central Los Angeles teacher who grew up in the tradition of the

Black church and faith-based social justice, was the first person who rendered me speechless.

"If Jesus were teaching in a public school today, I think he'd choose to work here," Melanie said. "These are the kids who need the most support—they are the forgotten ones in our society. So of course he'd come here!" She giggled a bit at her own presumption. After all (despite the proliferation of WWJD bumper stickers), who really knows what Jesus would do in any modern-day situation? But she certainly gave me something to think about.

When I taught in Compton, I definitely felt a sense of calling. While I didn't explicitly share my faith with my students, I felt divinely led to work in a challenging urban environment. I felt a responsibility to change my students' academic trajectory but also to let my life exemplify Christ's love, reconciliation, and justice.

To be honest, I still don't know if Jesus Christ would choose to teach in a poor urban school. But I do believe Christ would have a heart for the most challenging schools in our country. Why? The Bible mentions poverty over two thousand times and explicitly charges Christians to strive for justice on behalf of those who have the least power in our society. I cannot imagine a greater way to put these principles into action than to help 15 million kids growing up in poverty get the education they deserve.

Children growing up in low-income communities often encounter challenges that accompany poverty—including limited access to quality health care and healthy food choices, neighborhoods with disproportionately high crime rates, and overcrowded and underfunded schools. These children experience a unique set of challenges, some of which have a negative impact on their school performance. It's possible to view the numerous success stories of the previous chapter as anomalies; perhaps they are mere exceptions to an intractable rule.

Yet the Bible says that each of us is made in God's image and likeness. So regardless of a child's challenges or school conditions, Christians should realize that every child has potential. If we truly believe that God distributes academic potential across all communities equally, then we simply cannot stand by and allow children in low-income schools to fall further and further behind their wealthier, suburban counterparts.

But why are Christians uniquely situated to help solve the problem? Dozens and dozens of worthy causes knock on the church's door every day. Why should people of faith plunge into public education reform? Are we collectively charged to help improve low-income public schools? Is there a biblical argument for giving our efforts to help close the academic achievement gap, whether or not we see conversions to the Christian faith as a result of our efforts?

This chapter explores three interwoven scriptural themes that create a biblical framework for why Christians should respond to the academic achievement gap:

1. God's concern for children,
2. God's focus on the poor and disenfranchised, and
3. God's heart for justice.

I conclude this chapter by examining the biblical idea of human potential and the prophetic opportunity for Christians to champion high-quality education for all children.

Suffer the Little Children

God's love and compassion for children are crystal clear; we cannot argue against the value God places on the youngest among us. In Psalm 127:3 the Bible calls children "God's best gift" (Message). Christ repeatedly suggests that we need innocent, childlike faith if we want to fully understand God's kingdom (Matt. 19:14; 1 Pet. 2:2–3). Jesus reprimanded the disciples when they tried to prevent children from coming to him for prayer, and Jesus welcomed children with open arms (Matt. 19:13–15; Mark 10:13–16). He repeatedly warned us not to overlook the little ones or treat them with disrespect.

One of my favorite child-related illustrations comes from Matthew 18. When a disciple inquires about who gets the highest rank in God's kingdom, Jesus responds with a direct warning.

> Jesus called over a child, whom he stood in the middle of the room, and said, "I'm telling you, once and for all, that unless you return to square one and start over like children, you're not even going to get a look at the kingdom, let alone get in. Whoever becomes simple and elemental again, like this child, will rank high in God's kingdom. What's more, when you receive the childlike on my account, it's the same as receiving me. But if you give them a hard time, bullying or taking advantage of their simple trust, you'll soon wish you hadn't. You'd be better off dropped in the middle of the lake with a millstone around your neck. Doom to the world for giving these God-believing children a hard time! Hard times are inevitable, but you don't have to make it worse—and it's doomsday to you if you do." (Matt. 18:2–7 Message)

Yikes! My favorite line in this passage is "Hard times are inevitable, but you don't have to make it worse—and it's doomsday to you if you do." You have to love the Bible for its bluntness. Jesus doesn't mince words on this one.

We know that children are highly treasured by God, and we are explicitly commanded not to make their hard times worse. What do these commands mean for us in practical terms? How do we put these ideas into practice, particularly as they pertain to low-income public schools and the academic achievement gap? To help illustrate some key principles, we'll look at how two different churches implement their children's ministries. I use these two examples not to judge these churches—no church gets everything right—but to draw several important conclusions.

Church #1: Washington, DC

Our family belongs to a large, nondenominational church in the Washington, DC, area. We have three children (toddlers to teenagers), and we intentionally looked for a family-friendly church. Church hunting, one of my least favorite activities, became a full-time job. We know the perfect church doesn't exist (as one of my former pastors says, the perfect church ceases to be perfect the moment I walk through the doors!), but we did want a place where our children would feel welcomed, safe, loved, and valued. Alonzo and I were even willing to sacrifice some of our preferences (for me this means worship music that seamlessly blends acoustic Christian tunes with contemporary gospel music; for Alonzo it means sermons that pique all aspects of his intellectual curiosity), so that our kids could get what they need.

We eventually found a church whose children's ministry thrilled me, and now our youngest daughter looks forward to church with unbridled enthusiasm. The church has well-supplied individual classrooms for infants, toddlers, preschoolers, and lower elementary grades. When children arrive they can choose from a host of toys and crafts available for free play. The upper elementary room resembles a miniature Chuck E. Cheese, complete with a moon bounce so kids can burn off extra energy.

Of course, none of that matters if children don't receive excellent Bible-based teaching. Fortunately our church excels in that area, too. Every week after church our daughter regales us with the tales of what she learned. Her belief and knowledge of God grow every week, and she's having fun to boot!

We have electronic security equipment to facilitate the check-in process and to ensure that children get released only to their parents. During holidays every child sits in the main sanctuary with her or his parents, and ushers distribute a special packet complete with crayons, coloring books, and small, child-friendly Bible stories. Not surprisingly, the kids love every minute of it. Our church prioritizes children in its words and actions. And it puts its money behind those actions.

Church #2: Southern California

In contrast, during graduate school I worked part time at a large urban church. I oversaw the Christian Education department, which included adult education, teen ministry, and children's church. The incredibly diverse church welcomed about 10,000 worshipers each week, including 750 to 1,000 children who visited the Sunday morning children's church ministry while their parents and families worshiped in the main sanctuary.

Each Sunday morning brought a fresh, exhilarating undertaking! Our team welcomed children of all ages—from adorable toddlers to confident, question-everything middle schoolers. As the little ones received their nametags and gave their parents good-bye smooches (the toddlers, of course, and not the middle school kids), our team sprang into action. We had activities ready when children walked through the classroom door (eliminate idle time!); we implemented child-centered curricula as we designed crafts and object lessons for each age group; and we distributed the ever-popular snacks midway through the service with the precision of a Swiss clock.

As the church grew, our team looked for ways to continuously improve children's church. Several volunteers were full-time public school teachers during the week, so we naturally turned to effective teaching strategies: we implemented a rigorous orientation and training program for our volunteer teachers; we observed teachers in the classroom and provided feedback on their lessons; we reoriented our volunteers to move from activity-based lessons to a more objective-based curriculum. In short, our leadership team did our best to step up our game.

We were all volunteers, but we still took our work seriously. We felt a responsibility for the youngest members of our congregation, and we hoped each child had a superb experience that helped him or her feel treasured and esteemed. We wanted to demonstrate God's love and provide ample, biblically based teaching so that the children's interest about God would flourish. Most of us felt a sense of urgency, because we believed in a deeper purpose for our work. What could be more important than working with children?

I naïvely assumed everyone in the congregation felt the same way. Although Whitney Houston crooned, "I believe the children are our future" in her timeless ballad "The Greatest Love of All," I didn't always feel that vibe at my church. I remember feeling shocked and disheartened as I repeatedly stood before the church begging for more children's church volunteers. Why weren't people tripping over themselves to work with our future leaders? I enviously watched congregants line up to join the choir or the hostess department. These ministries displayed members' talents in front of the entire congregation. Perhaps our behind-the-scenes work didn't carry the same allure. Children's church could promote you to folk hero status among six-year-olds, or perhaps a few eleven-year-olds would occasionally say you're "pretty cool," but that was about it.

I once again convinced myself that the ancillary factors shouldn't matter. Didn't others sense that these little people were God's most precious resource? I kept my cool and told my team that we'd continue to pray for more volunteers. We stayed focused on our work and weren't deterred.

Unfortunately, the challenges did not disappear. We faced uphill battles on everything from space (we outgrew our rooms and held some classes in the hallway) to hosting special events (we canceled activities because we lacked sufficient funds). Over time my team and I began to feel demoralized.

I reached my crisis point during senior leadership retreat, where we discussed the church's vision and upcoming priorities. As in most organizations, the budget played a central role in our discussions. The senior pastor articulated an ambitious vision: the church planned to expand its radio and television ministries. It quickly became clear that ministry departments would be left to scramble for increasingly scarce resources. We each had an opportunity to make our fiscal case to the group.

I felt confident and ready to make a compelling case. The eternal optimist, I assumed it would be impossible to refuse the team that cares for our sweet, cherubic future leaders. Thinking strategically, I prioritized our most urgent needs based on which ones would not financially derail the church's other priorities. I decided to ask for chairs. Yes, I recognize that's pretty mundane. But we had run out of chairs for the middle school group and needed to rent more so everyone had a place to sit. Basic. Simple. Inexpensive. Who could turn that down? I made my pitch.

When I finished, the senior pastor looked at me for a moment and bluntly responded, "If I have to decide between chairs for the kids and new television cameras, you lose." The room fell silent. With the words "you lose" still hanging in the air, I glanced around at my colleagues and caught several sympathetic glances.

"Wow," I simply responded, "I guess that's pretty clear." And with that, the budget discussion quickly moved on, while another ministry leader pled her case. The church's top-down culture didn't foster the type of free and open debate that should have taken place in that moment. And I was too emotionally drained to push back. Despite the successes our children's ministry experienced, I increasingly felt like I was fighting an uphill battle.

Are Children a Priority?

Now, with a decade of experience behind me, I get it. I still don't like it, but I do understand. I also recognize that I judged the congregation members and the church leadership, when ideally I could have exhibited a more mature perspective. I believe that God gives each of us a specific calling and purpose. I know my passion and life's purpose centers around children, education, and justice. But not everyone shares that calling or my zeal. And that doesn't make them wicked. Just as someone who works to eliminate international human trafficking needs to aggressively push to get my attention, I should expect to do no less for the issues that God has laid on my heart.

These two church examples illustrate how children can become a priority and how easy it is for other priorities to overshadow the needs of children. Furthermore, kids are easy to overlook. After all, as some people say, "Children don't tithe, and they don't give offerings." Secular society offers a compelling parallel: "Children don't vote." Both statements illustrate the mentality often governing society's power dynamics, and children generally wind up on the losing end. Children's voices are arguably the most disenfranchised, in practically every sector of society. Maybe that's why God has such a heart for them.

What does it mean to have a biblically based, child-centric focus? A child-centered church honors the Bible's declaration that kids are God's "best gift," and it makes ministry with young people a top priority in time, energy, and resources. A child-centered church considers children in its organizational decision making, and it strives to meet their needs. If necessary, the church adjusts its agenda in order to take care of them—even if something else suffers.

I believe God's love and concern for children transfer to young people throughout society's systems and structures. It extends far beyond whether churches provide excellent care to children who come to weekly services or whether churches prioritize children's needs in their budgets. As Christians, we should ask ourselves: are we "making it worse" for children in poor communities—or are we part of the solution? Do our actions line up with the notion that children are a gift from God that should be treasured and well protected?

The academic achievement gap has a devastating impact on children. Neglecting educational disparities in public schools is akin to neglecting God's children. If we desire to align ourselves with God's biblical mandates, we cannot ignore the millions of poor children trapped in failing public schools.

Seeing the Poor and Disenfranchised

"My students are poor," declared Mark, a Christian teacher who works in urban Washington, DC. "Straight up. I really can't say it any other way. They have to deal with challenges that I'll likely never face in my entire lifetime." He became a bit sullen and quiet, as if reflecting on the disparity made him uncomfortable.

I encouraged him to continue. "Well, take one of the little girls in my class," he began. "She comes to school with a coat that has holes in the inner lining. When the wind whips up, I'm sure she can feel it blowing through her coat. At the beginning of the year she had, maybe, three different changes of clothes. Maybe. And they were all pretty worn out.

"I got to know her family during the year," Mark continued. "They live in a small apartment with their cousins and a couple of aunts and uncles. Maybe it has two bedrooms. But there must be about ten or twelve people living there. I'm guessing it's almost impossible for her to find a quiet place to study or do her homework. And she comes to school really hungry; she gets the free school breakfast and lunch every day. I'm not sure if she eats enough over the weekend."

Again, Mark fell quiet and looked out of the window. "She is such a sweet little kid. And she's incredibly bright and asks a ton of curious, insightful questions. But it's like no one notices that about her. It's hard for us to look past her dirty, raggedy clothes. It's almost like she's invisible. All we see is a poor little girl. But I know God sees more in her than that."

Mark's story says it all. Most students in low-income public schools are poor. God cares about the poor. And God commands us to work on behalf of the poor. Plain and simple. Those of us who have been blessed with more are expected to help those who have less. It's a fundamental principle for those of us who believe in the gospel. Consider just a handful of the more than two thousand Bible verses admonishing Christians to work on behalf of the poor:

> There are always going to be poor and needy people among you. So I command you: Always be generous, open purse and hands, give to your neighbors in trouble, your poor and hurting neighbors.
>
> Deut. 15:11 Message

> Never walk away from someone who deserves help;
> your hand is God's hand for that person.
>
> Prov. 3:27 Message

Don't walk on the poor just because they're poor,
and don't use your position to crush the weak,
because God will come to their defense.

Prov. 22:22–23a Message

Enter, you who are blessed by my Father . . . And here's
   why:
I was hungry and you fed me,
I was thirsty and you gave me a drink,
I was homeless and you gave me a room,
I was shivering and you gave me clothes.

Matt. 25:34–36a Message

These verses suggest that unless we support our brothers and
sisters who struggle in poverty, we cannot truly live up to the
Bible's mandates.

But Christ didn't simply support and help the poor. He made
a habit of proactively reaching out to the most forgotten and ridi-
culed people in society. He didn't just spend time with the wealthy,
well connected, and well established. He went out of his way
to help the men, women, and children whom others discarded.

In John 4:1–42, Jesus travels through Samaria en route to
Galilee. Tired and thirsty from his journey, he stops at a well
and asks a woman for a drink of water. The Samaritan woman
replies with shock: "You are a Jew and I am a Samaritan woman.
How can you ask me for a drink?" The verse continues with
the phrase "for Jews do not associate with Samaritans" (v. 9).

Jews simply don't associate with Samaritans; Samaritans
are considered beneath Jews in every way. Strike one. And all
women are considered beneath men. Strike two. Jesus does not
allow these societal constructs to faze him. He declares that he
is "the living water" (v. 10), and if she drinks of him (in other
words, learns his teachings and believes in him), she will never

again be thirsty. He chooses to reveal his divine character, the messianic promise, to a Samaritan woman.

Jesus further instructs the woman to "go and tell her husband" (v. 16) about the eternal promise just offered to her. But she claims that she doesn't have a husband. Jesus then exposes her sordid life story before she has a chance to reveal it: she's had five husbands and is currently involved with a man to whom she's not married. Biblical scholars believe that this woman was involved in an adulterous relationship. Strike three.

The Samaritan woman's adultery doesn't deter Jesus either. Others certainly cast her aside because she is a Samaritan and an adulterer, but he treats her with respect and concern. He demonstrates his unconditional love for her, and he helps her. He looks past her outward appearance and her personal story to see a woman worthy of his time and concern.

Throughout the Bible, Jesus continually reaches out to unwanted men and women. In John 8, he defends a woman caught committing adultery. The Pharisees want to stone her to death, but Jesus quickly turns the situation around and challenges everyone: "Let any one of you who is without sin be the first to throw a stone at her" (v. 7b). He takes up her case. He defends and protects someone that society rejects.

The list of outcasts goes on. Jesus heals lepers, among the most despised people in the Bible (Mark 1:40–45). He accepts a tax collector's hospitality, and the people angrily declare that Christ has "gone to be the guest of a sinner" (Luke 19:7). (Biblical era tax collectors were about as revered as our modern-day Internal Revenue Service.)

Obviously, children in poor communities are not lepers; nor are they adulterers. But I think it's safe to say that children living in poverty in the United States are often forgotten and ignored, just like the men and women Jesus befriended. As my friend

Mark suggested about his student, it's almost as though we don't notice them. Most of us likely have a brief sympathetic or emotional reaction to the idea of growing up in impoverished homes, but have we spent time with those children or empowered them with tools to escape poverty? Jesus's actions dictate, I believe, that Christians do the latter.

It's easy to forget about millions of American families and children living in poverty. But these children show up to public schools every day. It's tragic to imagine children, like Mark's student, coming to school hungry and attempting to focus on the daily writing lesson. It's heartbreaking to realize a twelve-year-old misses school because she needs to babysit her younger siblings while their mom searches for a new job. But that's what many poor families in America face every day. We cannot be the church God envisions unless we make a priority of issues that directly impact the poorest members of our society. Let's begin by improving public schools for the millions of children living in poverty in the United States.

Loving Justice

While it's one thing to help those in poverty, it's quite another to bring justice to the oppressed. And that's exactly where God's Word leads us. Christians must also seek justice for the poor. Let me use a school-based example to explain how I make a distinction between these two ideas.

If a church wants to help students in Compton, it might choose to donate boxed lunches to a needy, hungry student. While that would be well received and appreciated, that little girl's stomach will be hungry again at dinnertime. Will the church be able to meet that need as well? And what if she grows up, starts a family of her own, and still lives in poverty? That same church may need to provide *her* children free lunches twenty years later. How can we bring true and lasting justice to this child? And what does the Bible suggest we do?

The Bible does admonish us to provide direct services to the poor, as discussed in the previous section. But we're clearly told to do more. Every Christian has a duty to protect human beings from systemic injustice whenever and wherever we can. Examples throughout the Old Testament illustrate God's desire to eliminate unequal structures. In Exodus 23:10–12, God mandates that the children of Israel set up a "gleaning system" during harvest time. This ensures that the poor and vulnerable who do not own land can gather enough food. In Deuteronomy 15, God declares a year for canceling debts every seven years. In the seventh year, people are released from all their debts. Generational poverty wasn't possible under these structures because the Israelites had a built-in safety net. They had a great equalizer—as God intended it.

God's Word continually calls us to go beyond serving the poor. The Bible focuses on changing systems, structures, and inequities.

> Speak up for those who cannot speak for themselves,
>   for the rights of all who are destitute.
> Speak up and judge fairly;
>   defend the rights of the poor and needy.
>
> Prov. 31:8–9

> Woe to those who make unjust laws,
>   to those who issue oppressive decrees,
> to deprive the poor of their rights
>   and withhold justice from the oppressed of my
>   people.
>
> Isa. 10:1–2a

Is not this the kind of fast I have chosen:
   to loose the chains of injustice
and untie the cords of the yoke,
   to set the oppressed free
and break every yoke?

Isa. 58:6

Where do we see unjust laws and practices in education that perpetuate inequity and oppression? We will delve into education policy and systemic issues in chapter 9. But certain public education systems do reproduce inequalities. School district funding models, based on property tax revenue, generate more money for schools in wealthier neighborhoods with higher property values. Most school districts assign children to schools based on neighborhood boundaries. Even within the same school district, the quality of public schools can vary widely; these differences almost exclusively correlate with per capita family income. Wealthier families can afford to buy property in neighborhoods with better schools, leaving poorer families stuck in neighborhoods with failing schools.

Conceptualizing a biblical understanding of justice has proven difficult. The notion of justice often consists of radically different ideas among Christians. Should we expect all people to have equal opportunities in our society? And does equal mean "exactly the same"? If so, is that realistic?

To complicate the idea of justice even further, America is built on capitalism. Democracy, at its core, supports free markets and fosters (at least in theory) meritocracy: if you work hard, you will achieve. But is our public education system set up to truly foster a meritocracy? I believe we must improve low-income public schools; otherwise, our school system will continue to be the prime differentiator between students who achieve and those who don't.

We live in a free society, so we should never curb the extent to which parents can provide additional academic resources for their children. Parents can, and should, support their children's education as much as their financial means allow. But unless we help improve all public schools, we're eliminating millions of children from the opportunity to pursue the American dream. This type of systemic inequality, that disproportionately impacts poor and minority students, reeks of the very injustice that the Bible calls Christians to eradicate.

Human Potential

Besides supporting children and the poor, and working for justice, the Bible offers one more layer to create a biblical framework for Christians closing the academic achievement gap. Genesis 1:27 states that God made man and woman, and created them "in his own image." This powerful passage has amazing implications for us and how we view others. While the Bible does not fully explain what this concept means, most scholars and theologians believe God chose to make us with a unique capacity to reason, make moral choices, and experience an entire range of emotions and feelings. God also enabled us to connect to his greatness and power.

I also understand this passage to mean that we have, and are directly connected to, all the potential that God's infinite wisdom has to offer. Coming from the evangelical tradition, I realize that one could suggest that people tap into God's wisdom most effectively when they have a relationship with Christ. While that may be true, Evangelicals should not go into public schools, teach students about Christ and—only after they're connected to Jesus—help them get the education they deserve.

On some level, I understand why this seems appealing. But if we wait until everyone knows Christ before trying to bring about justice, we will wait a long, long time. More important, I think we would be missing the boat. God admonishes us through the Old and New Testaments that part of our responsibility is to work for justice while we're on the earth.

The potential for greatness does lie in each of us. Given this premise, how does God want us to view others? More specifically, what are the implications for how Christians see children in our nation's most challenging schools?

We can logically conclude that Christians should believe that every person has the potential for success. This isn't meant to imply that everyone will rise to the top of a field and become a neurosurgeon or a Supreme Court justice. What this biblical perspective *does* suggest is that everyone should have equal access to the "keys for success"—that is, every child should have access to an excellent education. Equal access to a high-quality education will allow any child to become a neurosurgeon—if that is what he or she chooses to do—because ultimately God distributes potential equally among God's children.

Our society should not perpetuate unequal systems and structures that limit certain groups of children from fulfilling their God-given potential. The current academic achievement gap suggests that children in wealthier communities are disproportionately more talented and gifted with greater academic potential. From a Christian perspective, is it possible that God—a God of equity and justice—would give middle-class children, upper-middle-class children, and White children an innate advantage to obtain the most powerful and lucrative positions in our society? The only answer, according to the Bible's teachings, is clearly a resounding No.

Evangelical Christians often champion the "sanctity of life." This phrase typically refers only to abortion. Many Evangelicals argue that a culture that allows legal abortions does not truly value human life. While many Evangelicals have fought against abortion for decades, we have yet to see a movement that expands the idea of "sanctity of life" to fighting for the "quality of life." If we truly believe that all life is sacred, then the logical conclusion is that once a life is born we continue to fight for that life to have equal opportunities to live up to its potential. This more expansive view of the quality of life is beginning to pervade some evangelical circles, but educational injustice doesn't generate nearly the same outcry that we hear over issues like abortion.

At the root of our country's two-tiered educational system is a belief system that is antithetical to biblical teachings about inherent potential. Many of the practices in our educational system go against the biblical evidence that all children are created in God's image and have great potential—regardless of race or socioeconomic class. Given the messages that our society sends through these practices, it's not surprising that educational disparity can seem intractable. As Christians, God requires us to embody God's perspective and push our thinking beyond society's messages. If God believes that all children have potential and promise, then we have the responsibility to envision another educational system that delivers equality for all. We need to envision an educational system that provides adequate resources, quality teachers, and high expectations for all children.

6

Motivating and Sustaining Faith

> It's been an absolute privilege. I know this sounds
> crazy, but I would do my job even if I didn't get paid.
> In fact, I sometimes wonder how could I have ever
> thought of *not* doing this? These are God's children
> and I am right where I'm supposed to be.
>
> —Aaron, a middle school teacher
> in rural North Carolina

I'd just hung up the phone after talking with one of my fellow
Teach For America alumni. As often happens from these conversations, I felt wonderfully inspired! The camaraderie and
esprit de corps among those of us who taught in urban and
rural public schools is unmistakable and not very surprising.
After all, we've gone through similar life-defining experiences.
Similar to when my husband's former Peace Corps volunteers
join us for dinner, my conversation with Aaron was peppered
with exclamations: "Oh, I completely understand that!" and

"Yup! That happened to me, too!" But Aaron and I share another unique characteristic: our faith and religious beliefs substantially motivated us to teach in low-income public schools.

In my role as Teach For America's vice president of faith community outreach, I was fortunate to meet with dozens of teachers like Aaron. Teach For America is not a faith-based organization, but young people from all religious backgrounds—including Jews, Muslims, evangelical Christians, Protestants, Catholics, Hindus, Sikhs, and Unitarians—flock to join the organization.[1] Why do people of faith find working in urban and rural public schools so compelling? These teachers do not explicitly bring their faith to bear in public school classrooms. They each strongly respect the separation of church and state. Nonetheless, the faith connection is organic, deep, and sustaining.

In this chapter we'll explore what motivates Christians who work to close the achievement gap in public schools. In spite of the inherent challenges, thousands of Christians embrace urban and rural public schools without the mind-set that seems to hold some Christians back from fully embracing this work (as discussed in previous chapters). What can we learn from their experiences, and how might their perspectives influence more Christians to get involved?

A Moment . . . Then a Calling

My colleague Aaron grew up in an upper-middle-class suburb and attended what he describes as an "awesome public high school." Aaron enjoyed a wealth of opportunities at his school, which was brimming with Advanced Placement classes, high academic expectations for students, and resources galore. From this privileged setting, Aaron said he could "write my ticket to where I wanted to go to college."

When Aaron arrived at the University of Texas in Austin, he said, he harbored a "naïve world view that assumed everyone had similar education and opportunities." He didn't understand affirmative action policies like the one Texas had recently adopted, which offered automatic admissions to all students who graduated in the top 10 percent of their high school classes.[2] He assumed the top students from low-income high schools were unqualified for college and were therefore taking admission spots from students at his highly competitive school.

Aaron's commitment to Christianity deepened during his junior year, causing him to explore how Jesus lived when he was on the earth. Aaron cultivated a profound desire to serve others and put other people's needs before his own, which is how he viewed Christ's example.

An elementary school in a low-income neighborhood near his college campus was scheduled to close because of chronically low academic performance. One of the teachers secured a grant to hire college-student tutors, in the hope of raising her students' achievement. This tutoring position appealed to Aaron's growing desire to live out his Christian beliefs, so he took the job. He quickly realized that several assumptions he'd made as a suburban teenager were wrong. Through tutoring children in a struggling low-income school, Aaron became painfully aware of the dramatic difference between his public education and the education of those he tutored. Affirmative action policies that had once appeared to Aaron as unfair seemed not only fair but also insufficient to address the drastic achievement gap Aaron now confronted.

It turns out that tutoring wasn't enough for Aaron. He applied to be a substitute teacher while still in college, because he wanted to make a broader academic impact on students. But unlike many of his fellow substitute teachers, Aaron regularly turned down substitute opportunities in wealthier neighborhoods. He wanted to work in only poor neighborhoods. He intentionally prioritized underfunded schools where students' reading levels were several years behind kids in richer areas. Aaron chose to teach in a setting where poverty's unfortunate consequences met him at the school door every morning. Toward the end of college Aaron realized that teaching in urban and rural neighborhoods was the perfect way to live out his faith. He wanted the honor and privilege of helping counter negative stereotypes that suggest that not all children can learn and achieve.

Aaron's work allows him to show the type of compassion that Jesus Christ showed to people of every background; he works to ensure every child has the opportunities God intended for all. Reflecting on the arc of his life, Aaron states, "God prepared me to do this, and my life was leading up to this moment." He decided to become a full-time public school teacher and hasn't looked back since.

Aaron's tale resembles many Christian educators' stories. When asked how they ended up teaching in low-income urban and rural public schools, they almost always describe a sense of being "called" to do the work, and they cite a deep Christian conviction to serve others and make the world a more equitable place. But they often also relate a seminal experience or a series of life-altering instances deeply rooted in their faith. It's what I call their "moment."

While Aaron's moment came from contrasting his own excellent public school with the low-income schools near his college, some of the teachers I've gotten to know experienced their moment earlier in life. Terrie grew up in a low-income community. The first of her family to attend college, she ended up at the prestigious and highly competitive University of Notre Dame.

During one of our conversations, Terrie reflected on how she felt during her college graduation. "I fully understand how monumental it was to achieve what I was doing," she began. "When I actually walked across the stage to receive my college diploma, I knew that no one in my family had ever done that before. It was pretty amazing. And I knew it would be a blessing for me to help others achieve their potential too."

Terrie's experience at Notre Dame fortified her moment. Her college years continually fostered a mind-set that service and social justice naturally extend from her Christian beliefs. After college she chose to teach fourth grade in an extremely impoverished, rural public school in Louisiana. She describes her thought process when making that life-changing decision: "I was wondering how I could make a contribution to the world and make a mark. As a Christian I felt I should help eradicate a social problem. And working in an urban public school fit perfectly with my desires and how I wanted to give back. Teaching was an amazing opportunity; it was, quite simply, a gift that fell into my lap."

Similar to Terrie, Brian experienced the academic achievement gap early in his own life. Brian, who eventually went to Pepperdine University and taught middle school social studies in urban Miami, grew up in inner-city Los Angeles. He attended ineffective urban public schools through eighth grade. His situation turned around when his parents moved to suburban San Fernando Valley. Brian got accepted to a magnet high school, which he credits with making all the difference for him. "My high school had totally different expectations from my middle school," he began. "The teachers motivated us, and they ensured we succeeded and were prepared for college. I was exposed to high-level math, science, and technology classes; the curriculum was 100 percent college prep. It was pretty tough to see my friends [who lived in urban Los Angeles] going to a very bad high school. Our high school education ultimately affected all of our lives. They went to community colleges or didn't go to college at all. And I got into Pepperdine."

Brian remained solemn for a moment and then continued, "It wasn't fair that I had access to something they didn't."

This unsettling dichotomy stayed with Brian as his Christian faith became a stronger part of his identity. Brian's college church connected Christian principles to a broader set of social issues, particularly those related to economic justice. Linking Christianity to injustice made perfect sense to Brian, particularly in the context of public education. He'd never forgotten the educational disparity he witnessed in high school, and he naturally connected those profound challenges to his ever-deepening biblical convictions. Brian describes a moment in which he realized he was experiencing "a convergence of everything that is most important to me." Similar to Terrie and Aaron, Brian saw helping close the achievement gap as a God-ordained step in his life's journey.

I love how God miraculously weaves together the stories of our lives. Each of us has a unique, personal history and God uses these experiences to bring us clarifying moments and define our calling. What can we learn from the moments that Aaron, Terrie, and Brian—and thousands more like them—have experienced? I would never suggest that every Christian should run right out and teach in urban Miami, rural Louisiana, or Compton, California. But I do believe these stories can inspire many more Christians to understand and embrace our own moments about low-income public schools.

How many of us have seen stories on the news about failing schools in inner cities? How many times have we heard a passing anecdote about the devastating high school dropout rate? Or perhaps, as presumptuous as this may be, someone reading this book may learn about the scope of the problem for the very first time. What will we do with our "moments"? I'm hopeful that we can learn to view the academic achievement gap in public schools through a biblical, faithful framework. Only then can we truly be a part of the solution.

It's a Justice Thing

As much as I celebrate the idea of feeling "called" to work in urban and rural schools, I recognize the limitations of this idea. When Christians or other people of faith proclaim that they feel called to work in low-income public schools, they can risk alienating communities they want to serve. When filtered through our own human frailty and ego, a calling can make us feel that we have something to do *to* the community. This places the importance on us rather than on the children who are stuck in failing schools. But when we couple our sense of calling with a strong desire to do justice—well, that's a different story altogether. This shifts the conversation to working *with* the community to improve student outcomes.

As we explored in a previous chapter, Christians—particularly Evangelicals—have become increasingly engaged in a broad range of social issues. Almost every Christian educator, principal, or education reformer I speak to couches his or her involvement with the achievement gap as a matter of biblically inspired justice. I believe this framework provides an important distinction that enables our work to become authentic and transformational.

Terrie's understanding of justice illustrates this idea. She contextualizes public school teaching as a way to work for change. "I'm called to be a disciple of Christ," declared Terrie. "For me that means I mold and shape my actions to the life of Christ. His greatest commandment was to love humankind. And I have to do the same."

I asked Terrie how this command relates to public education. She replied, "The issue of educational inequity compels you to serve youth and children. It's a way of extending the life of Christ by working with the community to improve it. It's connected to making the world a better place and bringing justice to those who don't have it. Justice, human dignity, and equality are inherently Christian ideals. Being a teacher has deepened my belief that faith and social justice are truly intertwined and inseparable."

Terrie's reflections represent a common theme among Christians who work in public schools. In 2010 *Time* magazine wrote a story about evangelical Christians working on public education issues. The piece, in addition to exploring why Christians are often drawn to working to close the academic achievement gap, contains one of my favorite examples of Christian-inspired justice. In the article Adam Brown, who taught in rural Louisiana, describes how his view of biblical justice deepened by teaching in a low-income community.

> "We talk about justice and mercy all the time," says Brown, referencing the oft quoted verse Micah 6:8. "But they're not the same thing. I went down [to Baton Rouge] thinking, 'These kids have gotta know that I could have gone into whatever and not be teaching down here in south Louisiana.' That they'd be grateful."
>
> Instead, Brown says, he's grateful to his students. "It's not about me giving them something they don't deserve out of the goodness of my heart," he explains. "That's mercy. This is something kids deserve and they just didn't get it like I did."[3]

I love this distinction! As Adam so clearly articulates, mercy is something that we just give people and, perhaps subconsciously, we don't feel like they truly deserve it. Perhaps we may secretly rationalize they should be grateful that we've taken the time to do something for them. How glorious it is when we can flip that idea on its head! Our efforts become about the children rather than our own sacrifice.

True confession: I was guilty of this sin of ego when I first began teaching. I assumed my students in Compton would automatically love and appreciate me, in part because I "made a sacrifice" to teach in a school where many educators didn't want to work. Not only was I incredibly naïve to think that ten- and eleven-year-olds would rush to embrace me (in any community, low-income or otherwise!), my semi-patronizing attitude ran the risk of making the work about me. A more mature teacher or child advocate realizes that this work is ultimately about the vast injustices students in poor neighborhoods face on a daily basis.

Education Is Fundamental

Just like every individual helping to make the world a better place, people of faith have to decide which social issues they will focus on. I'm obviously biased, but I believe a quality education has the potential to make a foundational impact on a person's life. Given the myriad challenges there and the many other social causes, why are some Christians drawn to public schools?

Poverty impacts millions of Americans. As discussed in chapter 2, poverty influences many aspects of a person's life, including quality health care and nutrition. Communities in poor neighborhoods experience disproportionate crime and rates of unemployment. While most educators recognize that society must confront these problems, they have come to view quality education as the foundational requirement to eliminate generational poverty. Simply put: education provides the pathway to future opportunities.

Adam, our teacher in South Louisiana, wrestled with how to have the biggest impact on poverty and injustice. During one of our conversations he reflected on why he chose to work in public schools: "I was planning to go to law school, but the statistics about the academic achievement gap compelled me to consider teaching. I visited some classrooms and started reading articles about education. I was overwhelmed at how deeply education is connected to all poverty issues."

Adam went on to explain that he initially thought law school was the most direct way to counter injustice and restore equity to the poor and disenfranchised. While he still believes in the power of the legal system, he came to view inadequate education as the root cause for many of society's ills.

Brian, who was raised in inner-city Los Angeles and went to Pepperdine, has a similar perspective but takes things a bit further. He recognizes that education determines future outcomes: "The quality of education that people receive is a complete differentiator. My students are getting behind academically, and that will affect the rest of their life. For some of them it will mean they may drop out of school, which can lead to criminal activities if they feel they don't have any other options. Education helps you find your purpose in life. It's connected to everything."

Brian recognizes an important factor: the further behind a child gets in school, the more likely he or she is to drop out before graduation. This correlation makes perfect sense. If children feel unsuccessful in school, they may lose their motivation to remain in a place where they experience failure on a daily basis. Brian believes that a quality education, and closing the achievement gap for students who are already dramatically behind, provide a fundamental life structure for all students—and particularly for students growing up in low-income communities.

We know that a high school diploma or a college degree isn't an absolute guarantee for future success. But the odds of succeeding without them diminish significantly. And while we can point to a handful of extreme outliers (e.g., Steve Jobs, Bill Gates, and Albert Einstein), the data don't lie. High school dropouts earn about $10,000 less each year than high school graduates and $35,000 less each year than college graduates. Over the course of a lifetime, a college graduate will earn, on average, $1 million more than a high school dropout.[4]

Christians working to close the achievement gap want to guarantee all children have an equal chance in life, and they believe an excellent education will help put children in poor communities on that path. While we know an outstanding school experience may not be the only thing that helps children achieve in life, it's undeniably a fundamental component. I believe people of faith will be more effective advocates if we embrace this premise. Otherwise, working on public school reform may appear tangential, rather than a key element to empowering children and families in low-income communities.

Against All Odds . . . Persevere

All of the Christians I've spoken to share a deep conviction that change is possible, in the face of seemingly unbeatable odds. These individuals will not quit, nor can anyone convince them that low-income children cannot achieve. Their bottomless faith encourages them to believe possible what others often find almost preposterous.

Let's return to Aaron, our teacher who grew up in suburban Dallas. He took a high school teaching position in a low-income, rural North Carolina high school. An engineering major in college, he was assigned to teach first- and second-year algebra and calculus. During one of our phone calls, Aaron reflected on his first weeks in the classroom: "I was so psyched to teach calculus," he recalled with a smile in his voice. "I figured I was getting the whiz kids. I planned to take them to advanced engineering workshops at local colleges and enter them in math competitions. But I quickly realized that was going to have to wait. After some initial diagnostic tests, I found out my students—the top math students at my high school—were only performing on a sixth-grade level. I was devastated."

Aaron wondered how his students, the most advanced students in the entire school, could be so far behind! How did this happen? And what could he do to rectify things? Aaron had to make a decision: would he let the status quo prevail and make mediocre progress this year—or would he try to move his students forward at an unprecedented pace? Was it possible to help seventeen-year-olds make progress when they were literally five or six years behind?

Aaron did some soul searching and decided to take a direct approach. He described how he confronted the challenge: "It was really tough. We had some frank conversations. I decided they were old enough and smart enough to think for themselves; I wanted them to be invested in their own success. So I told them they weren't on grade level to do even the basic math that's necessary for calculus. We talked about the factors that led up to this and how the situation got so bad. The kids decided that some of their math teachers weren't good—and so they'd learned to do what the teacher wanted so they would get a high grade. But it didn't mean that they'd actually learned the material. They'd just learned how to work the system."

I asked Aaron how the students responded to his direct conversation. After all, they'd been cruising through a system that, while it wasn't giving them a stellar education, they excelled in year after year. Aaron acknowledged the response wasn't overwhelmingly positive initially: "At first there was a lot of pushback. Students felt frustrated and, honestly, some of them felt as though they'd been scammed, you know? But ultimately we all agreed to move forward with some pretty ambitious goals. We motivated ourselves by realizing that they were setting the example for students who would come into advanced math classes after them. They could raise the bar for hundreds of students in the coming years. They got pretty psyched!"

Aaron's path with his students wasn't easy. Even though his students wanted to be challenged and pushed, it wasn't always comfortable for them. But he continued to motivate them by showing them their individual weekly progress and rallying them around the idea that they were setting the example for kids who would take calculus in subsequent years. And, not surprisingly, they rose to the occasion. The previous school year, students at his school were the third lowest performing on the state's end-of-year calculus exam. But that year, his students closed the gap between their test scores and the state average by 70 percent. Not only that, his class even outperformed many of the wealthier suburban districts.

Terrie, the first-generation college student who graduated from Notre Dame University, teaches nine- and ten-year-olds in rural Louisiana. As an African American southerner who didn't grow up wealthy, Terrie felt an immediate connection to her students. Similar to her before she went to college, most of her students didn't have a broad exposure to life beyond their small, rural community. They dreamed big, as she did as a child, but they were also scared and naïve.

Her students were, on the average, two or three grade levels behind in math and reading, and that had affected their confidence.

Terrie described in pained tones, "Many of my students suffer with crippling, relentless self-doubt. Even though they're relatively young, they've internalized wretchedly negative messages from past teachers, from the community, society, and peers. One of my students, a nine-year-old, said, 'You know I'm dumb and I cannot get this!'—and he meant it."

When I asked Terrie how she countered such seemingly engrained messages, she replied that the first step was to check her own beliefs. "Did I fully believe they were intelligent?" she reflected. "I had to be convinced, beyond a shadow of a doubt, that every student could achieve. Then, once I internalized that, it didn't matter so much what I said. But what mattered most was praising students consistently and making sure they saw small bits of academic progress. We tracked their results, so they could each see individual improvement—no matter how big or how small."

Adding another layer of complexity, Hurricane Katrina directly affected many of Terrie's students; over half of her class were transplants from New Orleans or Baton Rouge, and almost everyone had relatives impacted by the devastating storm. Terrie had to raise student achievement in the context of one of the nation's worst modern-day natural disasters.

Ironically, Terrie found a way to motivate the children by comparing them to a high-performing, well-funded school district: "The highest-quality school district in the state, Zachary School District, shared a border with our low-performing, economically struggling school district. Zachary was overwhelmingly White, and my students often received a glimpse of these fancy schools with amazing amenities. Many of the teachers at my school sent their kids to Zachary schools. The kids never talked about it openly, but they made remarks to one another to demean our school district: 'My mom said she's going to take me out of this crazy school district and put me into Zachary!'"

Terrie paused and laughed as she continued, "It was almost like Zachary represented the promised land for my students! But I decided to use that undercurrent. I chose to be transparent with each of my students about their progress. I shared exactly how much they needed to gain if they wanted to catch up to the affluent kids in Zachary. I was sure to convey that students in Zachary weren't inherently better or smarter than any of them. Every day I reminded my students they were brilliant; I had the utmost confidence in their abilities. And you know what? It worked. It took an insane amount of hard work, but the kids really progressed that year; all of my students made at least one and a half or two years worth of academic progress. Many students increased three and four grade levels that year!"

And how did her class perform against the wealthy school district? Terrie laughed and replied: "As a whole, they performed on par with Zachary kids in math. But they actually outperformed Zachary fourth-graders on the reading test. My students were so pumped! They almost couldn't believe it themselves. They kept asking me to double-check the score to make sure it was accurate."

Terrie choked up a bit as she continued: "That was the best day of my life. My students left that school year knowing they could do anything. They realized—and I became even further convinced—that it doesn't matter where you're born. Life circumstances don't have to dictate the end of your story."

And there you have it. Terrie and Aaron, along with dozens of other teachers I interviewed, believe deeply in the power of perseverance. Even when the circumstances don't suggest students can achieve, these teachers could not be swayed.

This quality of perseverance is not a uniquely Christian trait. Any successful teacher in a low-income school exemplifies strong determination in order to overcome the relentless obstacles on the path to closing the academic achievement gap. That said, if Christians want to improve low-income public schools, we must rely on the type of longsuffering that is described in the Bible. This work does not happen overnight. As Galatians 6:9 reminds us: "So let's not allow ourselves to get fatigued doing good. At the right time we will harvest a good crop if we don't give up, or quit" (Message). Amen and amen.

These teachers, and many others like them, provide an outstanding road map for Christians who want to understand how and why people of faith labor to improve low-income public schools. Their examples can help each of us listen to how we may be stirred to work on this issue and comprehend the extent to which education connects to a fundamental sense of justice. Above all, I hope we can internalize the sense of perseverance that highly effective teachers embody.

7

Closing the Awareness Gap

I hope that by now you are convinced that Christians *can* play a major role in helping to close the achievement gap in public schools. So far we've laid out the scope of the problem, delved into why educational inequity exists, and shown clear and compelling evidence that the problem can be solved. Chapters 4 and 5 explored a biblical framework supporting Christians' work with public schools and what has held us back from doing so. And the previous chapter illustrated why many Christian teachers have vigorously aligned their life's work to low-income public schools.

Given that, let's bring this down to the personal level. I hope by now you're asking some crucial questions, like: What exactly can I do? Where do I begin? How can Christians really help change things in public schools across the country? Is it more productive to work with public schools through my church? Are there concrete things that one person can do to make a difference?

Christians can engage with public schools in three important ways: *be a vision caster*, *become a laborer*, and *provide faith-based advocacy*. This chapter will explore the first way to become involved, and the next two chapters will explore the other two ways. When considering how we can engage with any major social issue, it's important to remember that we are all uniquely gifted. We are each likely better equipped and designed to tackle certain aspects of public education issues than we are others. Our congregations and faith communities have a variety of gifts and abilities as well as varying levels of capacity, so we need to present a multitiered approach to address these diverse capabilities. But don't worry! When it comes to fixing low-income public schools, there is plenty of work to go around. I'm confident we can find a way for everyone to get involved! This chapter, along with chapters 8 and 9, will help readers identify actions that they or their faith communities can do to help close the academic achievement gap.

Vision Casters

When I was in college, my campus pastor had a thing for purposeful vision statements. Several years before Rick Warren's international best seller *The Purpose Driven Life*,[1] my pastor had a healthy obsession with promoting purpose and vision. Every program and ministry had to be grounded in a clearly written vision—along with goals, objectives, and a concrete time line. While I was a fairly motivated child and teenager, college was the first time I'd been taught a systematic practice to establish a vision and create a concrete plan to accomplish my goals.

During my junior year, my pastor taught a series of compelling messages from the book of Habakkuk. Much of this short book (it's only three chapters) illustrates some rather intimidating wrath-of-God themes. But, in spite of the over-whelming amount of judgment verses throughout Habakkuk, I developed a fondness for these two verses:

> Then the LORD answered me and said:
> "Write the vision
> and make it plain on tablets,
> that he may run who reads it.
> For the vision is yet for an appointed time;
> But at the end it will speak, and it will not lie.
> Though it tarries, wait for it;
> Because it will surely come,
> It will not tarry."
> Hab. 2:2–3 NKJV

God commanded Habakkuk not only to *say* the vision but also to *write* it. This way many more people could read the vision, get inspired by it, and follow it. If Habakkuk got weary and began to doubt the vision, he also could return to the written vision and regain his hope and inspiration. My pastor's creative teaching genuinely brought this concept to life. I literally envisioned Habakkuk sitting down with his slab of concrete (for some reason I keep seeing flashes of Fred Flintstone chiseling a note for Wilma) and penning his God-inspired vision for the people of Judah.

In his context, Habakkuk's vision was one of bone-chilling judgment falling upon the people of Judah.[2] Nonetheless, I still found the idea of writing down a vision compelling. I wanted to spell out what I hoped would happen in my life—and I wanted to revisit those God-inspired promises over and over again.

Right around the time my pastor taught the Habakkuk series, I began keeping a journal; this helped bring tangible substance to my personal devotional time. I've saved dozens of journals from different stages of my life—including my undergraduate days, my years as a public school teacher, those seemingly never-ending graduate school years, and my life as a new wife and mother. These journals, which today are among my most treasured possessions, record the story of my life; the pages chronicle the highs and lows of my personal faith journey. I'm so grateful that my pastor taught about the importance of vision setting when I was filling up the pages of my first journal. As a result, I eagerly began incorporating vision writing into my journal time and have continued to do so ever since.

This contemplative practice provided remarkable clarity about what I believed God wanted me to do with my life as a college junior—and it still does, some twenty years later. I wrote vision statements to help determine my career path after graduate school; I annually update the vision for my professional, personal, and spiritual growth; my husband and I have even begun to think about vision setting for our family and each of our children. I refer to my vision statements throughout the year, and I do my best to have my actions line up with my deep core beliefs. When I struggle or feel defeated (which, as for most of us, happens on a fairly consistent basis), the vision reminds me of what I imagined. And, perhaps most important, vision statements bring me back to *what's possible*—even when I cannot see it anymore. I personally believe it's the first and most important step when trying to create something out of nothing.

So what does any of this have to do with Christians working to close the achievement gap in low-income public schools? I believe strongly that our nation desperately needs a clear vision for what's possible in our most challenging public schools. We need to write the vision, speak the vision, and declare the vision every chance we get. We need to change the prevailing narrative about urban and rural public schools. We have to proclaim the potential in order to counter the deep underlying questions about whether children from poor families can actually achieve at the highest levels. In short, Christians and other people of faith can play a crucial role as they join the small, but growing, chorus of visionary voices proclaiming that we *can* close the academic achievement gap.

If we are going to step into our role as vision casters, we have to inspire those within our sphere of influence to act. At a minimum, we can equip ourselves with a layperson's knowledge about the disparities in our nation's public schools. And then we can speak the truth about what's possible for children in low-income communities. Again, each of us has a different capacity and ability to influence others. Let's examine what this might look like. (And, trust me, it's not as intimidating as it may sound. You don't need a degree in education policy to become a vision caster, nor do you need to read a dozen books about public schools. Of course, either of those are certainly welcome—the more, the merrier!)

The Cocktail Party (or Coffee House) Circuit

When speaking at faith-based conferences and events, some of my favorite moments take place after the official talk ends; the microphones are turned off, and I get to hang out and chat with attendees. I often keep in touch with people I meet, particularly if I can provide some encouragement or advice for newbies trying on their vision-caster shoes for the first time.

One young woman I met after an event in Washington, DC, seemed particularly motivated to keep in touch. She was a college student actively involved in campus ministry groups, and she approached me to discuss how she might get involved with public education.

"I didn't realize things were so bad," Allison began with a sorrowful twang. "I mean, everyone knows that inner-city schools don't have a great reputation, but I didn't *really* know . . ." She drifted into silence.

I just smiled and nodded my head in agreement. I waited for her to continue.

"But, wow! Those stories of schools and teachers who help low-income kids learn so much in one year—I didn't know that was possible either! How come no one is really talking about that?"

"I think you're exactly right, Allison. We hear stories of success here and there, but we treat them as aberrations. It's almost like we think, 'Well, it's great that one or two extraordinary teachers or schools can help kids achieve at super-high levels. But there's just no way that's really possible for most kids in low-income communities.' We've got to transform the conversation so more people believe that all children can achieve regardless of their background—and then, subsequently, demand that all children achieve."

Allison was eager to figure out how she could make a difference on her college campus. We analyzed her available assets (idealistic young people, a strong social justice mind-set on campus, low-performing urban schools near her campus) and realistic constraints (lack of financial resources and lack of time—she and her friends were busy, overwhelmed college students). As we discussed what Allison might do as a first step, we realized that her biggest potential impact would be to get the conversation started among her friends and peer group. Her hope was that at least a few people that she interacted with would find a similar passion and then spark the conversation among their friends.

I've come to call this strategy the "cocktail party pitch" (or, for those who don't imbibe, feel free to call it the "coffee house chat"). Part of what makes this so appealing is that it cleverly disguises itself as a nonstrategy, while being surprisingly effective. Rather than randomly conversing with anyone and everyone on campus, Allison and I strategized how she might reach her most influential peers. Our theory, similar to what Malcolm Gladwell describes in *The Tipping Point*,[3] was that she would have a bigger impact by targeting key leaders on the campus who were uniquely positioned to influence a wide range of other students.

And what should Allison say during her cocktail party pitch/coffee house chat? We agreed that she should have a simple message:

1. Children in low-income public schools are performing significantly behind kids in wealthier school districts.
2. We know that they can achieve at high levels, because hundreds and thousands of teachers and schools see dramatic results every day.
3. What can Christians in our college community do to help change this?

She didn't have twenty detailed talking points, nor did she create a fancy PowerPoint presentation. She simply spoke about what she'd learned and brought it to life with compelling examples and statistics.

After the conference, Allison and I spoke on the phone every couple of months. In each conversation she regaled me with stories of how her casual approach created a mini-movement among her peers. While it wasn't a perfect strategy, Allison brought a fresh dialogue to her campus. Where public education and the achievement gap previously received very little attention at her school, she stepped up and spoke out for children stuck in failing schools, from the Bronx to South Central Los Angeles. When Allison's friends challenged and questioned her about whether or not the problem was solvable, she politely pushed back and stood her ground. She acknowledged that she didn't have all the answers, but she simply thought Christians should believe the best about kids who have the least in our country. She encouraged her friends to be a part of the solution.

Due to the interest she generated, Allison pulled together Christians engaged in other social justice issues to host a forum about public education and the achievement gap. I was thrilled when she invited me to her small campus to speak at the forum. Students asked many challenging questions about public school reform, and they definitely pushed my thinking! But several students decided to consider teaching in low-income public schools after graduation. And Allison helped spearhead a volunteer tutoring program at a public school near their campus.

Allison's story illustrates how each of us can proclaim a visionary message about our nation's public schools. Can you imagine the impact if thousands of Christians and other people of faith began to speak the same truth to our friends, families, and personal networks? And what if Allison hadn't felt charged to proclaim the good news about closing the achievement gap? How many students on her college campus would have missed the opportunity to become convinced that all children can achieve?

The Local Church: Small Groups, Sermons, and Seminars

Pastors, church leaders, and congregations can also build awareness about the academic achievement gap and cast a strong, much-needed vision for change. Local churches are a hub for information and have a unique ability to bring important issues to their members. Pastors can spotlight social issues in the context of biblical principles and expose their entire flock to fresh opportunities to work for change.

One of my colleagues wanted to find a way to get her small-group Bible study to take an interest in public education reform. Her weekly group included six women in suburban Chicago, with an equal mix of professional women and stay-at-home moms. We talked on the phone one afternoon and agreed that reading a book together would best spark conversation. We discussed several choices and settled on *Savage Inequalities*, Jonathan Kozol's classic book written nearly two decades ago, detailing the dramatic difference between public schools in inner cities and wealthy communities.[4] Its stories still have the ability to bring readers to tears.

The small group embraced the idea! They devoured Kozol's book and, according to my friend, got fired up with some pretty righteous indignation. She likened the group's metamorphosis to someone experiencing the loss of a loved one. First the women experienced shock and denial ("Things cannot really be this bad!" or "Is this really true? Kozol must be exaggerating!"). Next several members expressed intense guilt ("How could this happen right in our own country and I never realized it?"). Then they moved to anger and action ("Well, this is just insane! We have to do something about this!").[5]

Fortunately, after processing these emotions, my friend's small group did decide to do something. They didn't simply learn about the problem and stop there. The women wanted to impact their congregation by proclaiming the good news about what's possible in urban and rural public schools; they developed a vision to facilitate a church-based effort to support public education and low-income schools. They became champions for inner-city kids and encouraged at least a half dozen other small groups to read Kozol's book. They used a personalized approach to cast a vision for high-quality public education. As a result, the church began partnering with low-income public schools to provide tutors and classroom supplies for underfunded schools.

Small groups are just one way that local churches can build awareness of educational inequity. Several pastors and church leaders have asked my colleagues and me for suggestions about incorporating public education issues into their weekly church services. While I'm not a pastor or theologian, I am happy to provide church leaders with ideas. I believe the local pulpit can be amazingly influential when pastors and clergy discuss equity issues in a biblical context. Here are a few ideas that have worked particularly well:

- *Jesus, the ultimate teacher*—Church leaders can connect public education to Christ's role as the ultimate teacher. Jesus clearly valued high-quality teaching; it was an important part of his ministry, and he regularly used compelling illustrations and parables to instruct his disciples and followers. Clergy can challenge the congregation to strive for high-quality teachers in every public school. Pastors can invite teachers to discuss the impact they have with their students.

- *Education and justice*—Teach about educational inequity and the achievement gap in the broader context of the Bible's concern for justice and the poor. I don't know many other issues that fit as perfectly into a broader sermon about oppression and injustice. I encourage clergy to include statistics and stories about the academic achievement gap (see chap. 1 for examples). And, of course, I urge them to counter those statistics with stories of success.

- *Vocation in every sector*—Christians should have a presence in every sector of society. Our primary role isn't always to preach the gospel, but rather to illustrate God's love and concern for all humanity through our actions. Public schools should be no different. Pastors can highlight examples of Christians who make a positive impact on student achievement in low-income public schools.

- *A call to serve*—Clergy often charge their congregations to serve the most underprivileged and disenfranchised members of society. Pastors can highlight the needs in low-income public schools and encourage their members to get involved and be a part of the solution. Highlighting tangible examples of what Christians and other people of faith are doing can inspire others to serve.[6]

Finally, local churches can host mini-education events or invite external speakers to highlight the academic achievement gap and foster a vision for what's possible. I've seen several congregations do this, and it had a tremendous impact. A friend of mine, Aaron, leads a church in Washington, DC. The church rents a public school building for its Sunday morning services, and several church members teach public school in the city's most challenging neighborhoods. Aaron regularly invites teachers to address the entire congregation. The educators share their experiences, including their daily struggles and their success stories. These firsthand accounts sensitize the entire congregation to the challenges and possibilities for urban public schools. If congregations don't include teachers who work in low-income public schools, they can build relationships with teachers through other churches and then invite those teachers to come and share with their members.

Aaron also took things a step further and hosted a free screening of the documentary *Waiting for Superman*. The film, by Davis Guggenheim, chronicles several inner-city families seeking alternative public school options for their kids. While *Waiting for Superman* does not completely describe all the complexities of the public education system, it forces the audience to confront brutal inequities that low-income families confront daily. Movies like *Waiting for Superman* provide an excellent way to expose communities of faith to the academic achievement gap.[7]

Aaron invited me to the showing and asked me to introduce the film and provide some post-film comments. The screening, which took place in a historic movie theater near the church headquarters, was completely full! The buzz and excitement overflowed as dozens of people lingered after the movie to express their outrage at a public school system that relegates most poor children to a substandard education. The screening itself, which Aaron and his team had opened to people outside his church, helped inspire dozens of church and community members to take a more active role in the public education system.

Another church leader in Washington, DC, took a different but equally successful approach. Melanie's church included two staff members who focused exclusively on social justice issues. Several church leaders had children in urban public schools, so this issue was particularly relevant to the leaders. But they had not seen interest in public education across their entire church. Melanie hosted a public education forum after Sunday morning church services. Both the outreach director and the senior pastor agreed that people of faith should take an active role in closing the achievement gap; they believed the forum could light a spark among their congregation members.

I joined Melanie's congregation and spoke about my experiences working with low-income public schools. Melanie invited two other panelists—both of whom spoke directly to public education in Washington, DC. The three of us had quite a lively discussion! We didn't necessarily see eye-to-eye on the solutions for the district's public schools, but we did begin a new conversation in Melanie's congregation. Each of us carried a similar message: public school inequities may exist, but dramatic transformation is definitely possible. Similar to the viewers at Aaron's movie screening, the attendees left energized to take action on behalf of public school children.

Leveraging the National Pulpit

The local church is a crucial partner to help our country cast a different vision for public school achievement and equity. Beyond the local church, however, nationally influential pastors and faith-based leaders can provide another level of vision casting if they will champion public education as one of our nation's most important moral concerns.

The Christian community has national leaders who wield significant influence and can literally shift the narrative in thousands of churches around the country. If leaders like Rick Warren or Bishop T. D. Jakes champion a particular issue, they can generate significant attention and interest among Christians around the country. This approach has propelled issues like HIV/AIDS and global poverty to permeate the Christian culture. We need national faith leaders to take the same type of initiative concerning public education and the academic achievement gap.

Pastor Bill Hybels leads Willow Creek Community Church in suburban Chicago. Hybels also hosts the Global Leadership Summit, an international gathering of more than 100,000 Christian leaders around North America—live at Willow Creek and at a few dozen virtual sites around the globe. The Summit is one of the premier Christian conferences in the evangelical community. It promotes leadership development and gathers key thought leaders from both the Christian and non-Christian communities. Past speakers include presidents Bill Clinton and Jimmy Carter, British prime minister Tony Blair, Bono (from the musical group U2 and the One Campaign), CEOs such as Carly

Fiorina (Hewlett Packard) and Jack Welch (General Electric), and faith community leaders, including Pastor Rick Warren, Bishop T. D. Jakes, and Pastor Tim Keller.

Imagine my surprise when in early 2008, Bill Hybels's office contacted Teach For America's faith community outreach team, where I was working at the time. Bill had been following Wendy Kopp and Teach For America's approach of bringing top-notch leaders into urban and rural public school classrooms and had read Wendy's first book, *One Day All Children*, which chronicles the ups and downs of starting a successful nonprofit organization and social movement.[8] He invited Wendy to speak about educational inequity and the leadership lessons she learned as Teach For America's founder.

As a Christian, and a huge fan of Willow Creek Community Church and Bill and Lynne Hybels, I immediately recognized the significance of Wendy's invitation and the potential for impact. Our faith community relations team helped organize Wendy's visit and provided any relevant advice about the Summit's audience. We developed a plan to capture the Summit community's interest in education and Teach For America.

The morning of Wendy's talk at the Global Leadership Summit was one of the more exciting moments I've had since working on public education equity with faith-based communities. I remember sitting in the back of the sanctuary at Willow Creek as Wendy began her interview with Bill. I recall thinking, "Oh my goodness! Over 100,000 people are about to hear about the tragic education achievement gap in our nation—and Wendy is going to give them hope that the problem can be solved." What an opportunity!

Since Teach For America is not a faith-based organization, Wendy, like many of the speakers at the Global Leadership Summit, didn't address the achievement gap in a faith or religious context. She simply described the problem as a justice issue and suggested that educational inequity has a "moral dimension." Those two words deeply resonated with attendees, and her talk seemed to catch on like wildfire that morning and in the weeks and months that followed. Social-media-savvy audience members blogged and wrote Facebook posts about Wendy's talk, which fostered significant interest in education issues. Dozens of people at the Chicago conference site came to Teach For America's booth, some with tears in their eyes, and said they'd never heard anyone talk about public education that way—particularly making the case for solving the problem. I still meet people who remember Wendy's 2008 talk and declare that it fundamentally changed the way they think about the potential of all children, regardless of their socioeconomic or racial background.

I stayed in touch with the Global Leadership Summit staff over the next few years. I was again thrilled when Bill's team contacted us to ask for recommendations for other education reform leaders to speak at the 2011 and 2012 Summits. Michelle Rhee, the former chancellor of the District of Columbia Public Schools (DCPS) and founder of StudentsFirst, spoke at the 2011 Summit.[9] Although sometimes portrayed as a controversial figure in the education reform landscape, Michelle brings a much-needed "no excuses" message about education reform. And she did just that at the 2011 Summit. Michelle enthralled Summit attendees by describing her experiences leading DCPS, where she made several difficult and unpopular decisions, including closing underperforming schools and laying off underperforming teachers. When Michelle declared that she operates with an unfailing belief that all children can achieve—leading her to take actions she felt would ensure that all children in DCPS had a better shot at a high-quality education—the audience broke into spontaneous applause.

Bill Hybels and the Summit leadership continue to bring public education issues to the forefront; Geoffrey Canada spoke at the August 2012 Summit. Geoffrey founded the Harlem Children's Zone, which takes a comprehensive approach to education by supporting Harlem families with prenatal and early childhood programs, high-quality public charter schools, violence prevention programs, and medical services.[10] He has received numerous accolades for its ambitious approach to closing the achievement gap and breaking the cycle of generational poverty. Summit attendees gained another perspective about the possibility for change through Geoffrey's presentation.

By the end of 2012, the Willow Creek Association will have singlehandedly highlighted the vast public education disparity for more than 300,000 Christian leaders over the course of three Global Leadership Summits. Tens of thousands of Christians can bring Wendy's, Michelle's, and Geoffrey's visions about educational equity to their own churches and faith-based networks and begin to take action. Bill Hybels's commitment to educational equity and public education reform is clear. I am so grateful for national Christian leaders who continually build awareness of this issue!

Other national Christian leaders have taken similar steps to cast a vision for a biblical perspective on public education equity. My friend and colleague Noel Castellanos leads the Christian Community Development Association (CCDA). Founded by the legendary civil rights leader Dr. John Perkins, CCDA supports local Christian ministries to help restore and empower underserved and underfunded communities. Dr. Perkins and Noel demonstrate a true heart for children in low-income public schools. Many CCDA members work and live in poor neighborhoods, so the issues often impact their lives directly.

Noel and I first met through a mutual colleague at a faith-based social justice conference at Princeton University, and we kept in touch over the years. I was delighted when Noel reached out to me in 2010 to talk about public education and how CCDA could incorporate education issues throughout the organization. After several conversations, Noel informed me that their board had agreed to make public education one of CCDA's signature issues in 2011. I could hardly contain my excitement when Noel shared the news! I couldn't imagine many Christian organizations better poised to impact public education and the achievement gap.

In October 2011 more than 4,000 faith-based community leaders gathered in Indianapolis for CCDA's annual conference. Education reform played a central role in the plenary sections and workshops. I had the opportunity to address these leaders, along with a few other educators, and speak about my experiences teaching in low-income public schools and championing public education reform. In addition to keynote speeches, CCDA's workshop sessions included several focusing on education reform; the conference's annual Justice Film Festival included numerous education-focused documentaries and feature films. CCDA plans to build on the momentum it established in 2011 by continuing education reform conversations in smaller city-based settings. I look forward to seeing the outcomes!

I'm grateful for national faith leaders like Bill Hybels, John Perkins, and Noel Castellanos who are bringing education issues to the forefront of our community. I pray that others will follow their lead.

Becoming Vision Casters

We have described several ways in which Christians can help raise awareness about educational inequity:

1. *Individuals*—We can influence those in our immediate circles by educating others and ourselves about the scope of the achievement gap and by sharing compelling success stories.
2. *Churches*—Churches can speak about educational inequity from the pulpit; small groups could study the issue further by reading books on the topic; and churches could sponsor seminars or education-related events.
3. *National leaders*—National faith-based leaders have significant influence throughout the Christian community. We should encourage them to wield that influence to help improve low-income public schools by speaking about the achievement gap in national venues, writing op-eds, or highlighting public education at their conferences.

Christians and other people of faith can embody prophetic leadership roles and "write the vision" about what's possible for children in low-income public schools.

8

Laborers in the Movement

Then He said to His disciples, "The harvest truly is
plentiful, but the laborers are few. Therefore pray
the Lord of the harvest to send out laborers into
His harvest."

—Matt. 9:37–38 NKJV

In the previous chapter we looked at one way Christians and
people of faith can get involved in the public school reform movement, and that was by being vision casters—inspiring others to
join the movement. In this chapter we will discuss a second way
to become involved, and that's by becoming a laborer directly
in a school or through a support organization.

There's nothing quite like a farming reference to inspire Christians to run right out and work with low-income urban public
schools! But as much as modern-day agricultural analogies don't
fully resonate with the 84 percent of Americans living in urban
or suburban areas (according to the 2010 United States census),

I do love Jesus's words to his disciples: "The harvest truly *is* plentiful, but the laborers *are* few" (Matt. 9:37 NKJV, emphasis added). He essentially tells them that there is a lot of hard work in front of them, but the harvest (the reward) will be phenomenal. He tells them that if they're going to reap that reward, they will need more laborers. He promises a large harvest, but he also tells his disciples that they need more people to do the difficult, not-always-so-exciting work. And that's exactly what we need to help improve public schools and close the academic achievement gap for millions of children—we need a lot of laborers. Once we *educate* and *inspire* others to join this movement (as discussed in the previous chapter), we need to get to *work*.

Recall that in chapter 3 we described a number of schools showing significant academic success among their students. I describe more success stories in this chapter, but specifically focus on groups that are *motivated by their faith*. I highlight effective schools, teacher training organizations, and chuch-school partnerships, and illustrate detailed actions that people of faith can take to improve low-income public schools. While we have yet to build a cohesive, comprehensive movement for change, thousands of Christians are engaged in school improvement efforts around the United States. We'll explore what these efforts look like—from communities of Christian teachers in public schools, to churches that start public charter schools, to churches that support public schools by providing academic resources. We will seek to understand not only *what* these Christians do, but also *how* and *why* they are working to improve public schools in poor communities.

Teaching in Public Schools

Teaching in a public school classroom is one of the most direct ways we can become laborers in this movement. It may be a cliché, but it's difficult to imagine any way to have a more direct impact on the academic achievement gap. As described in chapter 6, many people of faith already teach in our nation's public schools. These teachers don't overtly share their faith in the classroom, but they are motivated to work in challenging low-income communities, in part, because of their Christian beliefs.

While teaching isn't for everyone, I certainly encourage anyone who expresses an interest in classroom teaching to pursue it. College students, mid-career professionals, stay-at-home parents, and recent members of the military can all find a pathway to teaching in low-income schools. Future teachers can go through a traditional teacher education program at a college, or they can apply for one of the many alternative programs that support non-education majors who've already received an undergraduate or graduate degree in another field.[1]

Training and Supporting Effective Teachers

David Montague runs a unique teacher preparation program. David is an unlikely candidate for urban school reform. He spent several years at an investment firm and then worked for Campus Crusade for Christ in Eastern Asia. When he returned from that venture, a friend encouraged him to join a local Memphis foundation focused on improving low-income public schools. The foundation decided to create a faith-based teacher corps, and David, who desperately wanted to make a tangible difference in the world during the second half of his career, jumped on board as the founder and executive director.

David leads the Memphis Teacher Residency (MTR), a cohort-based program that enlists young professionals to teach in Memphis, Tennessee's low-income public schools. David exemplifies sincere dedication and commitment to improving low-income public schools. I first met David through a mutual colleague who immediately recognized the synergies in our respective work. When we finally had a chance to speak over the phone, I was thrilled to meet another kindred spirit.

I asked David why he chose to focus his efforts on the achievement gap. I found his response captivating. "I often tell people that 'need is the new opportunity,'" he began. "I used to pursue lucrative opportunities, but now I pursue need. I want to constantly ask myself, 'Where are society's biggest needs, and how can I help meet those?' I believe the Bible is less about how humans can get into heaven and more about God coming to earth and providing us with a road map to reclaim and restore lives and institutions. He wants us to help make every system and structure into his ideal image. I cannot imagine a system more in need of that type of transformation than America's urban public schools."

David's organization, MTR, is part of the broader nationwide Urban Teacher Residency United network. Applicants go through a highly selective application process. Those who are selected for the program commit to working in a low-income public school for four years. During the first twelve months, the teachers are official "residents," similar to the training experience that medical doctors receive. They take courses, engage in group discussions and reflection exercises, and work at a school as an apprentice with a master teacher. The apprenticeship evolves from observing, to co-teaching, to teaching portions of the entire class by the end of the school year. After the residency year, cohort members commit to teach at least three years in the district.

What makes David and the Memphis Teacher Residency unique? It's the only faith-based residency model in the nation.

MTR has a unique, explicitly Christian identity. The organization's website states: "The mission of the MTR is to positively impact student achievement in Memphis' urban schools by recruiting, training, and supporting outstanding teachers, all within a Christian context."[2] MTR strongly believes in the importance of a quality education and views the academic achievement gap as our nation's "single greatest social justice and civil rights" violation. This language resembles what most education reform organizations champion, but MTR puts this in a faith context, as they further explain their mission: "We believe, that all students can learn and all students—as those made in the image of God—have amazing potential for a life . . . potential for spiritual and emotional success; and potential for living this life with purpose."[3] And, not surprisingly, MTR strongly believes in the power of teachers. They cite numerous research studies that show teachers are the single most important differentiator of student achievement within the school context.

David and his team provide a unique Christian experience for each of the cohort members. He shared about MTR's "Christian Community Education" idea: "We endeavor to prepare responsible and highly educated teachers, and we're motivated by biblical kingdom values. These values require us to provide all children, regardless of race, class, or religion, fair and equal access to basic civil rights such as K–12 education. Additionally, these motivations provide the opportunity for teachers to live their career as a calling to bring fairness and justice to all of creation."

David went on to share that MTR teachers do not have to be Christians; the program is open to everyone. So while some teachers may not be Christians, Christian principles do undergird the program's belief system. David likened it to the faith-based principles under which many hospitals operate. A hospital may align itself with Catholic or Baptist beliefs, which undergird their ethic of care, but they employ people of every faith or of no faith. MTR believes deeply in the idea of working in community to support one another, which derives from Christian teaching. They encourage their teachers to live in the communities where they teach, modeling the Christian idea of incarnational living.

How does an explicitly Christian organization train teachers for public schools, given the distinct line that's been drawn between religion and public institutions? David and his team have a no-tolerance policy when it comes to teachers overtly sharing religious beliefs with students. The teachers who choose to join MTR understand and respect the separation of church and state; they believe their *actions* demonstrate God's love as they labor to bring all students the education they deserve. David further explains this idea in a *Christianity Today* article.

> Public education is a promise by the government to every child in America that you can get a quality and free education at your local school. For a child to get a great education, they have to do that within a healthy and safe environment. If you're a Christian and you're using your classroom as a means of sharing the gospel, you have just destroyed the healthy and safe learning environment for any child in your class that is Hindu, or Muslim, or Jewish, or atheist.[4]

As David so eloquently articulates, any Christian wanting to successfully impact the public school academic achievement gap must relinquish all desire to use the classroom as their personal pulpit.

Even if Christians do not become classroom teachers, we can still find other ways to support public school teachers. Our much-needed support can still directly impact a child's education through our prayers, compassion, and financial resources. The following story illustrates exactly how these actions can positively impact teachers.

In 2011 I received an invitation to speak at a large, community-based church in Los Angeles. The Dream Center, led by Pastor Matthew Barnett, is strongly committed to the local neighborhood; it sponsors, among other things, an after-school program, a drug rehabilitation center, and a mobile medical clinic.

After I spoke at the church, Pastor Matthew prayed for all parents in the congregation who desired a better education for their students. Dozens of parents stood up and seemed delighted that the pastor acknowledged their unique struggle. Then he asked all the public school teachers to make their way to the front of the church. Seven or eight young people, looking slightly bewildered, walked down the aisle. The pastor personally thanked each teacher for his or her enormous sacrifice, commitment, and hard work. Then he asked the congregation to pray for the teachers. I was so touched witnessing these educators begin to weep as they felt the congregation's love and concern embracing them.

Most congregations would stop there, and there's certainly nothing wrong with prayer (I don't know too many teachers who will turn down extra prayers!), but Pastor Matthew took it a step further and decided to give each teacher a small financial gift. He asked his congregation to collectively donate a thousand dollars to each teacher. "It's a gift," he explained. "We want to honor you for what you do every day; you work graciously for lower salaries than you deserve. You can take this money and spend it on your classroom or, perhaps, just do something nice for yourself. It's totally up to you."

The teachers' eyes widened in disbelief, as they began to laugh, cry, and hug everyone around them. I had the chance to catch up with a couple of them after the service. We chatted for a bit about what I shared with the congregation and what they received that night. One young woman summed up everything quite succinctly: "I never imagined my pastor would single out teachers. I know to some people a thousand dollars may not seem like a lot of money, but to me, it feels like a million dollars. It's not the money; it's what the money represents. My church respects what teachers do, and I will always appreciate that. I don't know of any other church that's done what happened here tonight."

There are other ways Christians, congregations, and faith-based organizations can support teachers and classrooms. Consider getting involved with organizations like DonorsChoose, who connect prospective donors to teachers' classroom "wish lists." DonorsChoose facilitates a type of matching program, similar to a wedding gift registry, where donors search the organization's website to find a teacher they want to support, then purchase much-needed supplies for his or her students.

Faith-based organizations or churches can use their outreach and mission funds to donate to nonprofits with a proven track record of providing high-quality teachers to urban and rural public schools.[5] Nonprofit organizations like the New Teacher Project and Teach For America train high-quality teachers specifically to work in low-income public schools. These organizations predominantly rely on private donations to accomplish their goals. How great would it be to see thousands of congregations raise offerings in support of public school teachers? We can set an inspiring example by demonstrating a true commitment to hardworking educators in our nation's most challenging schools.

Starting and Supporting High-Quality Public Schools

Leadership matters in every sector. It's an indisputable fact. It's no wonder that thousands of books and articles, from the *Harvard Business School Review* to *Christianity Today*, write about the elusive high-performing leader. What makes her or him excellent? How can we replicate their traits and teach them to others?

It should come as no surprise, then, that school leadership matters. Numerous research studies demonstrate the impact a high-quality school leader can have in terms of turning around an entire school's academic trajectory. And some of the most effective models of closing the academic achievement gap are found at the school-based level, where, inevitably, a highly effective leader is at the helm. Considering this, how might Christians get involved with school-based leadership—either directly or through a supporting role?

As national charter school laws allow more flexibility, faith-based organizations and churches have begun to open public schools in low-income communities. This model provides an interesting opportunity for faith communities to get involved in public education. In some states, congregations and faith organizations can start public charter schools that are affiliated with the organization but do not have an overtly faith-based agenda. Starting a school is certainly not for the faint of heart; it requires relentless determination.

Esperanza Academy High School, a public charter school in Philadelphia, represents this trend and provides an interesting model of how faith communities can become laborers in the movement to improve low-income public schools. Esperanza High, founded in 2000, is a part of the larger Esperanza organization, which is a faith-based network of more than 12,000

Hispanic churches and faith-based organizations in the United States. Esperanza has significant influence within the Latino community and in the nation. It has gained distinction for hosting an annual Hispanic Prayer Breakfast in Washington, DC The breakfast highlights key policy and social issues impacting the Hispanic community, including quality housing, economic revitalization, and comprehensive immigration reform. (And it hasn't hurt that Esperanza's prayer breakfast has secured the president of the United States as its plenary speaker for the last several years.)

A couple of years ago I had the privilege of meeting some of the leaders who founded Esperanza High. We instantly developed a camaraderie based on our mutual interests. After one of our conversations I received an invitation to tour the school. I readily accepted and scheduled a visit during my next trip to Philadelphia. I made my way to the school via train, subway, bus, and foot, and eventually found my way to Esperanza Academy High School.

Esperanza High sits in an area known as North Philadelphia, one of the city's poorest neighborhoods. While some smaller parts of North Philly have recently begun to see the economic gains that often accompany gentrification, the majority of the community suffers with high unemployment and minimal retail or industry investments. Most of North Philly's residents are African American or Puerto Rican.

Students living in the North Philadelphia neighborhoods, sadly, reflect the traditional academic achievement gap found in most low-income communities. One neighborhood, Strawberry Mansion, reflects the broader achievement gap throughout North Philly. A nonprofit organization working to bring a school-home partnership to the area noted the following statistics.

[Sixty-six] percent of adults in our zip code area do not have a high school diploma and 96 percent lack a bachelor's degree. The average SAT verbal score for students attending neighborhood high schools is 300 points (out of 800). Additionally, just two years ago, more than 75 percent of the students in our neighborhood who actually graduated from high school failed some portion of the annual standardized test administered state-wide that spring.[6]

Reverend Danny Cortés, the school's chief administrative officer at the time, met me at the front door with a warm welcome. We spent the remainder of the morning talking about the successes and challenges Esperanza High has experienced as we toured the entire facility and popped into several classrooms. With a healthy sense of the realities of urban education, I am deeply impressed with all that Esperanza accomplishes.

By the numbers, Esperanza High regularly exceeds the surrounding public schools' academic outcomes. Esperanza's graduation rate significantly outperforms the local public schools; almost 90 percent of its students graduate on time. Close to 85 percent of its graduates are accepted into colleges and universities and attend right after high school.

Before leaving, I asked Danny why Esperanza originally launched a public school instead of a Christian school. For an overtly faith-based organization, it almost seemed more natural for it to start a school where teachers have the freedom to talk about their religious convictions. Danny simply replied, "We wanted to start a school that everyone in the neighborhood can attend, regardless of whether or not their families can afford it. A private school tuition bill would have prohibited the vast majority of our current families from attending. We think *this* is the work of the church; we should help provide all poor and minority children access to a high-quality public education that doesn't cost them anything extra."

Danny also directed me to listen to the words of Reverend Luis Cortés, the founder of the entire Esperanza network and one of the most prominent Hispanic faith community leaders. Luis recorded a video spot for the faith community outreach campaign that accompanied the education documentary *Waiting for Superman*. The "We Are Not Waiting" campaign sought to mobilize people of faith around educational inequity during the documentary's 2010 release. In the video clip (which also includes reflections from former congressman Reverend Floyd Flake from New York, Reverend Tony Campolo, and Geoffrey Canada), Luis and Danny eloquently retell a story that moved them both.

> During one of our student groups at church, we had a young lady who was graduating from the local high school struggle to read the Bible. She was graduating at the top of her class, but she was functionally illiterate. That was the moment we decided to start a school. And of course we had people tell us not to do it; the naysayers said it would be too hard. And it was definitely the hardest thing we've ever tackled. But we want to create a new culture. An institutional culture, an educational culture.[7]

Esperanza's work illustrates a phenomenal example of how Christian communities can work to start and lead successful public schools that literally change their students' life prospects. Again, starting a public charter school is incredibly challenging; this work isn't for everyone. And charter schools, which are still a relatively small number of public schools (and certainly not all of them are effective), are not the magical answer that will close the achievement gap. But I highlight schools like Esperanza Academy High School as proof of how communities of faith, through a lot of hard work and with expert advice, can help improve public education in low-income communities.

What are other ways that Christians, churches, and faith-based organizations can support high-performing school leaders and high-quality schools? People of faith can provide financial support to organizations that do these things en masse. New Leaders for New Schools, for example, has recruited, trained, and supported more than eight hundred public school leaders in low-income communities since 2001. These training schools consistently outperform their peers when comparing student achievement, graduation rates, and college matriculation data.[8]

Numerous churches and faith-based organizations have begun to directly support high-performing public schools, in some cases by providing space for these schools as they're getting off the ground. One of the highest-performing public schools in the District of Columbia, the KEY Academy, got its 2001 start in a church basement in the Anacostia neighborhood. KEY has long since outgrown the church's space, but what a wonderful legacy for that congregation. They had a foundational role in launching a school that's closing the achievement gap for hundreds of students every year.

The Pan African Orthodox Christian Church (PAOCC) has a particularly unique partnership with the KIPP Liberation College Prep in Houston. A public charter school, KIPP Liberation partnered with PAOCC to create a school-based program aimed at Black youth development. And the church donated land for the school to be built on. The church's leadership believes deeply in the church's role to support quality education.

"Black people have more churches, more preachers, more choirs than any other people, and still our people are in the greatest trouble. We've got to raise a generation that can think, a generation that chooses school over drugs, jobs over prison. It's the church's mission to be the mother of the black community," the Holy Patriarch says. "The problems in the black community are too great for 'business as usual.' We've got to make a difference now."[9]

The Houston congregation found a direct and concrete way to support high-quality education in their local community. I believe their model represents a new and cutting-edge way that churches can support public education.

Church–School Partnerships

According to the most recent United States census data, there are over 322,000 churches in this country, compared to about 98,800 public schools.[10] And when we look at the number of those schools that meet the definition of "high poverty schools," we're down to about 44,500 schools.[11] Our country has more than seven times as many churches as it does high-poverty public schools. Seven times as many! That raises the question, What can individual churches do to help ensure children in these public schools achieve at the highest levels?

As I mentioned previously, our family attends a large, non-denominational, family-oriented church in the Washington, DC, area. As I began to look for opportunities to serve in the congregation, I was drawn (not surprisingly!) to our community outreach efforts. One Sunday our senior pastor announced that the church leadership desired to impact the local community in a new way. We'd had a long-standing relationship with an impoverished village in Nicaragua, and our church embraced Rick Warren's P.E.A.C.E. plan, which focuses on five "global giants" that the church can help eliminate around the world. But the leadership team asked a pointed question: if our church disappeared tomorrow, would our neighbors even notice? In other words, how are our actions contributing to positive change?

How are we helping to feed the hungry and help the homeless down the street?

I met with our outreach pastor, Mike, to learn more about the work the church was beginning. I was excited to learn that our church's outreach ministry would include a focus on public education through a partnership with a low-income public school near our church. The church agreed to adopt one school and work with the school officials to support the teachers, their students, families, and the community to help provide a meaningful contribution to education, a positive learning environment, and relational support. I asked Pastor Mike why, given the myriad of other community needs, the church should develop public school partnerships.

"We want to embody what the Bible describes in John 1:14. I particularly like the way *The Message* says it: 'The Word became flesh and blood, and moved into the neighborhood,'" Mike began. "Our church wants to embody that idea of 'moving into the neighborhood.' That's how we can become relevant and truly begin to meet others' needs. And what better place to do that than the local public school? Residents may go to different shopping malls, churches, grocery stores, and gas stations. But they are all brought together at the neighborhood public school. The school is a place of community in a neighborhood; and if the students in that school are struggling . . . that's where we want to be."

And so our church began to build a relationship with a public elementary school about fifteen minutes from our church. The elementary school is a Title I school, which means that a significant percentage of the families live below the poverty line.

About a year and a half into the partnership, I sat down with Pastor Mike again to get his reflections on how things have progressed. Always affable and encouraging, Mike had such positive feedback on the public school partnership; he referred to it as one of the highlights in our congregation's local community outreach portfolio.

Mike said that the church began the conversation with the elementary school by simply asking what the school needed and if we could be helpful in some way. "It was challenging," Mike revealed, "because we certainly had ideas of what we might like to do based on what other congregations have tried and our church members' interests. We wanted to fill backpacks and donate school supplies to the kids. But I quickly heard the school leadership say what I've heard from other entities serving low-income communities: 'We don't need another of this or another of that. Let me tell you what we really need.' And so we stepped back and truly listened. Subsequently, our initial plans changed."

Our church eventually agreed to support the school with the church's food program; that was the most pressing need and something our congregation could support. We collected food, boxed it, and brought it over to the school on our designated weekends. And things took off from there.

Several months later we learned that many parents at the school either couldn't read at all or couldn't read English. The faculty identified this as a crucial stumbling block in their efforts to build student literacy. Parents are important partners who reinforce what students learn in school, but illiterate parents struggle to do this. During a meeting with the principal, the assistant principal, two third-grade teachers, a guidance counselor, a parent liaison, and two other staff members, Pastor Mike again asked the staff what they needed to help combat the parent literacy challenges. The school wanted to host adult literacy courses for parents who cannot read. So our church, which already had a partnership with a literacy program in our county, started holding classes at the school.

The school also wanted to do a community event, where families could spend time getting to know one another outside of school, but they didn't have the resources to pull it off. Our church stepped in to help meet that need as well. We cooked and served a sit-down spaghetti dinner for several hundred parents and children. To make the event more family-friendly, we hired several photographers to take free family portraits, so each family would leave with a beautiful family photo.

Spaghetti Picture Night grew the following year, as two hundred additional people (and a few more photographers!) joined the festivities. Our church wanted to add an academic component to the event, as we constantly kept the end goal of increasing student achievement in mind. The principal appreciated our willingness and suggested that we collect books—not for the school library, but for families to take and build their own home libraries. Children who have books in the home are likely to increase their reading comprehension at significantly higher rates than those without books.

The church set a goal to collect two hundred new books, which seemed quite ambitious. We involved the entire congregation, as well as the Christian school that is affiliated with our church. We clearly underestimated what our church could do, because in the end, we donated more than 950 books to the school! Every family at the event enjoyed a delicious meal, received a beautiful family portrait, and left with at least six books for each child. This was clearly one of Pastor Mike's happiest moments with the partnership. He enthusiastically declared, "I wish everyone could have seen the kids beaming from ear to ear when they got their handful of books!"

The public school partnership continues to blossom. Our church sends volunteers every week to tutor children in reading, and we continue to host adult literacy sessions and donate food to needy families. Recently, we helped convince an Apple supplier to donate several iPads to the school. Good things are happening, and I have no doubt they will continue!

My most recent conversation with Pastor Mike took place on the afternoon when the NASA space shuttle *Discovery* was scheduled to fly over the Washington, DC, area. In April 2012 the DC area ground to a halt as most of us clamored for a place to watch *Discovery*'s last hurrah as it rode piggyback atop a 747. Mike was scheduled to tutor his two mentees that morning, right as the shuttle was due to cruise the DC skies. Being a self-proclaimed space enthusiast, he called the principal to see if he could get parental and school permission to take the kids offsite for their tutoring session, hoping that they could also glimpse the shuttle. Mike knew this request was a long shot, but he figured it wouldn't hurt to ask. Not surprisingly, the principal said they couldn't permit that.

At the risk of missing a piece of NASA history, Mike showed up to tutor his children that morning. While this may not seem like a particularly large sacrifice, it did actually sway one extremely skeptical teacher. This teacher had been very reluctant when our church began a school partnership, because she "didn't believe the church should be involved with public schools." But two years later when Mike missed the shuttle flyover to tutor his students, that same teacher told him she was impressed that he put the students above seeing *Discovery*. She told Mike, "I never would have thought someone would do that for our students." It took a couple of years of showing up and being present, but this teacher eventually came to believe the church's motives were pure and truly about the children. (And, for those of you fellow space aficionados, don't worry: the school principal did some fancy coordinating and ushered the entire student body and faculty to the school's playground at just the right moment to view the shuttle. Pastor Mike ended up getting a picture-perfect view of the shuttle with hundreds of cheering students and teachers—which was infinitely more fun than anything he could have planned!)

From speaking with Pastor Mike and several other congregations that have begun partnerships with low-income public schools, I believe we can take away several key lessons of what works and what doesn't.

Meet the Need

Find out what schools need, and meet those needs. Period. While I understand the temptation to dictate what we see as their needs, that approach isn't likely to get congregations very far. The school leadership, teachers, and parents know what they need. They are there every day and we're not. If a school says they don't need something, don't do it. Don't make assumptions about a school's need without talking to the leadership. I've heard dozens of stories of church-school partnerships run aground because congregations didn't pay attention to this first and crucial step. Also, let's not forget that communities of faith may initially be viewed with skepticism. One way to overcome that is to approach a school as a humble listener. And humble listeners don't set the agenda; humble listeners find a way to meet pressing needs.

Leave Your Agenda at the Door

A companion to the first point, agendas (whether hidden or overt) have no place in church-school partnerships. Given the church's tumultuous relationship with public education during the last sixty years, we need to pay particular attention to this point. I cannot think of a better way to ruin a church's potential to help a low-income public school than by secretly hoping to infiltrate the school for the purposes of proselytizing the students, families, or faculty. Trust me, they know if you're trying to do it. For those who feel compelled to share their faith with others, there are places for that. A church-school partnership just isn't one of them.

Build Authentic, Trusting Relationships

We're not going to get anywhere without strong relationships. If we want to do this well, we need to be patient, because these relationships will take time to develop. In our era of instant gratification and technology that presents information in less than a nanosecond, this can be challenging. We want everything to move quickly, but we'll need to exercise patience. Churches build credibility by taking time to get to know the school community and doing the little things well. Otherwise, we run the risk of schools not ever really trusting the congregation to help with mission-critical initiatives.

On the flip side, church members don't want to feel as though they're serving in the context of a "transactional relationship." One church leader I spoke to said his church didn't take the time to develop real relationships with a public school, so their work ended up feeling more like what he termed an "ATM partnership." The church met a few financial needs for the school but never really built the type of trusting relationships that would have fostered a much deeper and long-lasting partnership. In one telling account, the school called this particular pastor to see if the church could help with a teacher appreciation luncheon. The church agreed to supply the food and, of course, wanted to attend the luncheon to socialize with the teachers and faculty. Unfortunately, they hadn't built real relationships with the school, so the principal informed the church that they didn't think it would be appropriate, since the teachers didn't really know anyone at the church. Not surprisingly, his congregation eventually lost interest in the school partnership, and it folded.

Build on Existing Relationships, If Possible

While this isn't always possible, churches should look to build partnerships where they have an existing "in" at a school in a low-income neighborhood. My church built a partnership with a school where our outreach pastor's wife had worked for more than a decade. That gave our church a certain amount of initial credibility. We still had to do the hard work of building trusting relationships, but that preliminary connection certainly helped. If church leaders do a quick assessment of their congregation, I'd be willing to bet that someone in the pews works at a low-income public school, sends their child to a school in a low-income neighborhood, or knows someone who does.

Cultivate a Network of Champions at the School

Churches find it helpful to build relationships with multiple stakeholders on school campuses, given the fluctuating nature of public school leaders and staff. Not only does this allow for continuity if a key staff member leaves the school, but it also helps build more investment and support for the partnership.

Have an Eye toward Student Achievement

Every school in low-income communities has a plethora of needs, and churches will likely feel compelled to meet each of them. At the end of the day, I encourage churches to prioritize their support for programs and activities that help increase student achievement. There is certainly a need for congregations to support schools with social services, but that tends to be where many churches start and end their support. As congregations build relationships with the school leadership and faculty, continually ask about ways the church can support student learning. Ultimately, we want to help close the academic achievement gap.

Effective church-school partnerships take a true commitment and willingness to build long-term, sacrificial relationships. Two Christian organizations that have spent considerable time wrestling with how to develop effective partnerships with public schools are 20/20 Vision for Schools and the National Church Adopt-a-School Initiative. Both organizations model many of the best practices for effective church-school partnerships, and they provide helpful resources for churches interested in starting partnerships with public schools.

Incarnational Living

During graduate school, like most habitually broke students, I sought the least expensive housing option possible. Fortunately, one of my fellow students at UCLA opened her home to me (rent-free, I might add!). Melissa and her husband, Tom, worked for World Impact, an urban Christian ministry. They lived in a low-income, mostly Latino neighborhood in central Los Angeles. As missionaries, they raised their own support and lived a life relatively free of material extravagance.

As an African American woman who grew up in an urban, working-class neighborhood, I'll admit that this idea of people choosing to move into communities that many of my peers and I spent years trying to leave struck me as odd. Is it possible to do this in a way that doesn't come off as paternalistic or reeks of "White Knight Syndrome"? For the millions of Christians who already live in a low-income community every day, this strategy may sound strange as well. Ultimately, I believe that Christians, regardless of where they live, should build authentic relationships with those living in historically disenfranchised communities and ensure the people living in the communities are truly empowered to drive the necessary change in their own public schools.

Having said that, the two years I spent living with Tom and Melissa were among the best that I spent in Los Angeles. I marveled that highly educated Christians, who could likely secure good jobs, would choose to live in a poor community where they were the Caucasian minority among predominantly Latino neighbors. Melissa worked with World Impact's Christian elementary school down the street from our house, and Tom ran the technology department for the organization. Let's face it, there is a certain amount of political, social, and economic capital that people like Tom and Melissa wield that, if used in a humble and appropriate manner, can support community change in a unique manner.

I quickly saw how their intentional decision yielded untold returns. While their work was significant and contributed in real and important ways, they both built authentic and meaningful relationships with their neighbors that had nothing to do with their jobs. Tom and Melissa were invested in the community in a personal way because whatever happened in the neighborhood impacted them too. I saw a completely different experience from what most of us do (myself included): we definitely sacrifice while we "do service," and then we return to our comfortable homes, cities, and countries.

I learned more about genuine, humble, servant-based Christianity during the two years I lived with Tom and Melissa than I could have ever learned through a thousand well-crafted, perfectly researched, fancy, church-preached sermons. I believe it was an experience that God allowed me to have so I could envision a different type of Christian commitment.

Incarnational living, or intentional living as it's sometimes known, has gained popularity in certain Christian circles during the last ten years, in part due to the ministry of Shane Claiborne. For those unfamiliar with him, he's a dreadlock-wearing, carbon-footprint-reducing, wardrobe-making, White Christian man who has chosen to live in inner-city Philadelphia. As a White man with dreadlocks, he's already going to stand out pretty much everywhere he goes. But choosing to live in urban Philly? He definitely attracts attention, albeit unintentional. Shane has a deep commitment to incarnational living, which is the idea that Christians can uniquely represent God's love and compassion by living in community with those they wish to serve. Shane cofounded the Simple Way, which is a network of Christians who choose to do just that: live simply and always in poor neighborhoods.[12]

The idea of incarnational living has interesting implications for how Christians may choose to become involved with low-income public schools. In April 2012 *Christianity Today* wrote its first-ever cover story about Christians and schools.[13] The article explores the varied educational options that parents choose for their children, including homeschooling, Christian schools, and public schools. The story also highlights a group of Christians in Richmond who purposefully moved to Church Hill, a low-income, predominantly African American neighborhood. Similar to Tom, Melissa, and Shane, none of these families share the racial or economic background of their neighbors.

Christianity Today's article details how the friends made a commitment to moving into an urban neighborhood, but several felt challenged when it came time to make school decisions about their soon-to-be-kindergarteners. Would they choose to send their children to the relatively low-performing neighborhood public school, or would they find an alternative, such as a charter school or homeschooling? As one of the men put it, "What would it communicate to our neighbors if we said, 'We're moving into your neighborhood, but we don't consider your schools and public institutions good enough for our families'?"[14]

Christianity Today's article highlights other families who've made similar choices. Stephanie McLeish and her husband moved into a low-income New Orleans neighborhood. McLeish, along with several urban families, contemplated starting a Christian school but ultimately chose to send her children to the neighborhood public school, where her son is the only White student in his class. She explains her decision:

> In the end . . . many of us felt this was an excellent time for the church to engage the public schools of our city. . . . Christ is at work redeeming all things, not just souls but also places, systems, business, and even education. . . . The problems as well as the blessings of living in this impoverished community have become my own.[15]

The article illustrates the honest, difficult thought processes and decisions that these families went through when choosing to send their children to the local public school. The parents did not take this decision lightly, nor did they come to it easily. Like each action step highlighted in this chapter, incarnational living isn't for everyone. Shane Claiborne acknowledges this when he's often asked if all Christians should do what he's doing.

> There are certain things we can say are clear Gospel mandates—like caring for the poor and sharing the salvific love of Jesus with others. But Jesus doesn't tell everyone the same thing when he invites them to follow. [To] one person he says, "be born again." Another he tells to sell all they have and give it to the poor.

There is an unmistakable call in Scripture to "not conform to the patterns of the world." . . . But just because we are called to be radical non-conformists doesn't mean that we all end up doing the same thing. Nonconformity doesn't mean uniformity. We are all called to carry a cross, but that doesn't mean all the crosses look alike.[16]

The one nuance that this article doesn't highlight is the hard work of public school reform that takes place every day among families who do not have a choice about where they can send their children to school. They have no other options. Some of these parents have been fighting to improve their children's schools for years, many of them motivated by their faith. So while it's wonderful to celebrate the parents who choose to move into local communities, we must acknowledge that the really hard work comes from families who have been there all along.

For those who feel called to move to low-income urban and rural neighborhoods and send their children to public schools, it can have incredible rewards. This approach allows Christians to become true partners with the community and collectively work for change in struggling public schools.

Other Ways to Support Public Schools

I'll conclude this chapter by highlighting an amazing example of how churches and faith-based organizations can support public education. The Dream Center, the same Los Angeles church that gave public school teachers a monetary gift, also presented their neighborhood public school with a phenomenal gift. I first heard about this church and its commitment to public schools when attending a gathering of Christian leaders in Washington, DC. The forum highlighted how people of faith are addressing some of society's major social challenges. Used to being the only person in the room talking about public education and the achievement gap, I shared my story and enjoyed listening to my fellow attendees' stories.

Much to my surprise, another faith leader stood up and described his church's work with a low-income public school. Pastor Matthew Barnett shared how he'd become compelled to do something to improve public schools near his church. The Dream Center, as I described earlier in this chapter, has a strong commitment to the low-income, urban community surrounding the church. Pastor Matthew explained that the church leadership became increasingly convinced that providing children with a strong education was fundamental to eliminating many of the systemic social problems the church worked to solve.

Not knowing how The Dream Center could best impact local schools, Pastor Matthew and a couple church leaders looked up neighborhood public schools on the internet. They identified one particular elementary school with high poverty and low student achievement and went to meet with the principal. Matthew described the initial meeting as going something like this: "We didn't really know what to do, so we went to the principal and told her that we were from the local church and wanted to do whatever we could to help the school. The principal seemed a little taken aback, and somewhat unsure about what we wanted. I reassured her that we truly didn't have an agenda; we simply wanted to be a blessing to the school. So I asked her what the school needed and that our church would like to take an offering and donate it to the school. For whatever you all need."

I appreciated Pastor Matthew's honest, humble approach to the school. He didn't approach the principal with anything in particular. He asked what they needed, rather than telling her what the church wanted to do for them.

"The principal told us that the school needed new computers so they could use technology to improve instruction for kids who were at wildly different reading and math levels," Pastor Matthew continued. "So I told her that we'd share their need with our congregation and take an offering for the school. The principal was cautiously excited, but I always wonder if she was thinking, 'Okay—I'm sure we'll never hear from these folks again!' Over the next two weeks our church raised $50,000 for the school's computers. I wish you could have seen the faces of the teachers and the principal when we brought them a check. Some of them literally wept with tears of encouragement and appreciation."

That is the church at its best. I'm so grateful for church leaders like Pastor Matthew and others who have found creative ways to support public schools. We need many more laborers if our nation is going to eliminate the academic achievement gap.

9

Faith-Based Advocacy

How terrible it will be for those who make unfair laws, and those who write laws that make life hard for people. They are not fair to the poor, and they rob my people of their rights.

—Isaiah 10:1–2a NCV

"That seems so political," a pastor replied during a conference in California. I'd just laid out a case for why Christians should get involved in education policy. I asked him to share a bit more about his reluctance. "I just don't think Christians should get very involved in policies that are ultimately determined by politicians and legislators. Every party has positive attributes; but they will inevitably demonstrate some corruption too. I'm all for churches helping schools, but championing certain education policies and aligning ourselves with politicians? I just think that takes things too far."

In the previous two chapters, we saw how people of faith can participate in the movement to close the academic achievement gap by becoming vision casters or laborers. In this chapter we will explore a third way to participate in the movement, by providing faith-based advocacy.

I certainly understand the reluctance that some Christians experience when considering education policy advocacy. Beyond the fact that wading through the murky waters of education policy reform is complicated for anyone, throwing a religious framework in the mix can render it seemingly impenetrable.

However, I believe there is a path for Christians and other people of faith in the education policy and advocacy arena. Throughout this chapter we will explore the following ideas:

1. Why public education policies represent an important lever in the fight for educational equity,
2. A Christian framework for policy advocacy, and
3. Why some Christians are reluctant to work on policy issues and how we can begin to move beyond these barriers.

This chapter concludes by identifying some general education policy areas in which Christians should consider becoming involved and some general resources to get you started.

A French Aristocrat, an Ohio Mother, and Education Policy

What do Victor Hugo's *Les Misérables* and an African American single mother in Ohio have in common? And how can both help us wrestle with a biblical definition of justice within the context of education policy? Both illuminate gut-wrenching realities that sometimes cause law-abiding individuals to blur the lines between what's legal and what seems morally permissible. Both stories call out a set of distinctly unequal systems and structures. Their dilemmas illustrate fuzzy shades of gray and present interesting case studies for Christians who want to understand and deconstruct a biblical definition of justice through the lens of laws and policies.

Les Misérables is a familiar tale. In nineteenth-century France, the story's protagonist, Jean Valjean, is arrested for stealing a loaf of bread in order to feed his sister's seven destitute children. Valjean spends several years in prison for his crime. After his eventual release, the plot takes us through complex themes of social inequity, justice, mercy, and fairness. We are forced to wrestle with whether or not Valjean's original sentence was just. After all, Valjean was simply trying to take care of his sister's starving children. The kids had no other apparent options and presumably would have starved to death. Should we grant leniency to Jean Valjean, given the circumstances?

Let's consider the modern-day story of Kelley Williams-Bolar, a single mom in Akron, Ohio, who gained national attention in 2011. Williams-Bolar raised three children in Akron's public housing projects. As in most inner cities, quality schools are sparse in Akron, and the local neighborhood public schools are among the worst in the area. According to state data for 2008–2009, only 48 percent of African American students scored at or above proficiency in reading, and only 39 percent scored similarly in math.[1]

Knowing the life-changing importance of a good education, Kelley made a decision to send her children to live with their grandfather in nearby Copley-Fairlawn School District. Her children were never official residents of Copley-Fairlawn, so Kelley technically broke the law by using her father's address to send the children to Copley-Fairlawn. In 2011 she was convicted of two felony charges for falsifying records and sentenced to ten days in jail, three years of probation, and eighty hours of community service.[2]

Adding to the tragic irony, Kelley is an assistant special-education teacher at an Akron district high school and a student at the University of Akron, where she was one semester away from receiving her bachelor's degree and teaching certificate. Now that she has a felony conviction on her record, the presiding judge, Patricia Cosgrove, informed her, "You will not be allowed to get your teaching degree under Ohio law as it stands today." This mom was trying to do the right thing. She was working hard, balancing life as a struggling single mother to get her college degree so she would have the means to move her children to a neighborhood with better educational opportunities.

Fortunately, Kelley's story didn't end there. A national grass-roots movement engulfed her as more than 180,000 people signed an online petition demanding that Ohio's governor, John Kasich, grant her clemency. In September 2011 that's exactly what happened. Kelley has expressed remorse for her actions and has now become a local leader in public education reform.

I've found that reactions to this story generally split into two camps. There are those who feel strongly that this mom was in the wrong and "got what she deserved." On the flip side, the vast majority seem to feel that she was justified and shouldn't be punished. I find degrees of truth in both arguments. According to school enrollment restrictions, this mother certainly did break the law.

But ultimately I believe that an "either-or" perspective on Kelley's story misses a deeper and more significant opportunity for reflection and societal change. I believe we should be asking ourselves a key question: Why do we create systems that force people to make dire ethical choices about basic human needs, such as food or a decent education? As a Christian, I believe

God wants us to look at adverse and unjust situations in our society—such as educational inequity—and realize that we have the opportunity to truly make a positive impact. And that, my friends, is where education policy becomes central.

My husband and I are fortunate to have wonderful, high-quality school options for our three children. We will likely never face the ethical choice Kelley had to make. But under similar circumstances, would I make the same decision she did? Would I feel pressured to ensure my children got the best education possible, even if it meant bending the rules to do it? Honestly, I'm not sure. Kelley knows what we all know: the best way to ensure our children have an equal chance in life is by providing them with a quality education. She was willing to take a risk to make that happen.

As Christians, instead of passing judgment on Kelley and other moms in similar situations, we should focus our efforts on understanding why our nation's unequal public school system drives some parents to break the law to ensure their kids get a good education. More important, what can we do to help change our country's overall public education policies so parents won't have to face such dire choices? Is it possible to envision and work toward a different reality?

Public education policy, like the one that prohibits children from attending schools outside of their neighborhood boundaries, has a tremendous impact on parents like Kelley and, in some cases, limits the educational prospects for their children. The answer, in this instance, isn't necessarily to allow every parent to send their children to any school across the state (there are some basic practicalities that render that solution virtually impossible), but there are nuances and unintended consequences with this particular law (a common practice in practically every school district across the country) that yearn

for a faithful advocacy voice. Millions of children are trapped
in failing schools because of neighborhood boundaries. What
policies should states and school districts create to counteract
these inequities?

The Expectations Project

The Michelle Rhee era in the Washington, DC, metropolitan
area raised more rancor and divisiveness within the education
reform community than I have ever seen. Michelle Rhee, as chancellor of the District of Columbia's public schools (2007–2010),
came into the city with a definite sense of urgency to close the
achievement gap. Michelle had never run a school district before, but she had led the New Teacher Project, a highly effective
nonprofit that works closely with urban school districts around
the country. Handpicked by DC mayor Adrian Fenty, Michelle
received his full support to embark on several aggressive reforms, including closing schools, dismantling teacher tenure,
instilling teacher merit pay, and creating a teacher evaluation
system that included student achievement as one measure of
teacher effectiveness.

In short, Michelle went after some of the most entrenched
structures in public education. America's teachers' unions, the
National Education Association, and the American Federation
of Teachers have millions of members and even more money.
Michelle (and other reformers holding similar views) is generally viewed with disdain (that's probably putting it mildly) by
union leadership.

While I don't have space to detail Michelle's entire District of
Columbia journey in this book, suffice it to say that Michelle's
reform agenda, and what some would characterize as her less-
than-endearing relationship-building approach, left behind a

trail of lovers and haters.[3] Mayor Fenty lost his 2010 reelection bid largely because of Michelle. Residents either cheered or wept when Michelle resigned shortly after Mayor Fenty's failed campaign. Depending on whom you ask, Michelle's departure was either the greatest thing since the invention of the cell phone or the complete and utter demise of public education in Washington, DC.

The truth probably lies somewhere in the middle, but Michelle can be credited with sparking a national debate about public education policy and reform. What I noticed, however, is that Christians and people of faith were largely absent from either side of the debate. Where are the faith voices in this new and burgeoning education policy debate? Why aren't we speaking out about education policy? Can we help bring more civility to the rancor and divisiveness that abounds within the education reform debate?[4]

In Fall 2011, I left Teach For America's national staff to start a new nonprofit organization, The Expectations Project. We had made significant inroads into faith communities through building national partnerships with faith-based organizations, but we realized that people of faith could be engaged on broader education issues in addition to supporting Teach For America's mission. My colleagues and I believed public education reform was almost a completely untapped area.

The Expectations Project's mission is to help engage Christians and people of faith in the broader movement to eliminate educational inequity, seeking to build a network of faith-motivated advocates. We want people of faith to work and serve in their local public schools, but we also hope to bring people of faith into the public education reform conversation.

We anticipate accomplishing two other key objectives through The Expectations Project. First, we want to build bridges between racial groups and between individuals from diverse economic backgrounds. Many of the current education reform conversations happen either without voices from the communities most impacted by the academic achievement gap (e.g., African American and Latino low-income families), or the debate is drawn along racial lines. Neither approach (whether perceived, actual, intentional, or unintentional) helps secure support for important reforms. Education reform cannot transform low-income public schools without working alongside, respecting, and fully engaging the families in the schools.

Cross-cultural race relationships are challenging in any context, even among those who share the same overarching faith beliefs, but I am optimistic that people of faith can help bridge some of these racial divisions. The Expectations Project will work tirelessly to ensure our coalition represents diverse voices. We hope that by uniting racial groups under our common beliefs we can successfully work with communities most impacted by the achievement gap.

The Expectations Project also strives to operate with a deep commitment to civil discourse. We believe there is much room to find common ground within education reform, and when that cannot be achieved, we will adhere to the motto of "disagreeing without being disagreeable." At the end of the day, our society must prioritize disenfranchised children; we don't have time to watch the "grown-ups in the room" argue with one another. Every day that the education reform community wastes on arguing and name-calling is another day that children in Compton, the Bronx, and Detroit won't learn to read, build critical thinking skills, or excel at calculus. These rancorous divisions are completely counterproductive and limit our ability to work collaboratively. People of faith are not perfect by any means, but The Expectations Project strives to bring a different type of voice to the education reform table.

Christians and Policy Advocacy

The Bible makes a fairly clear and compelling case for Christians to mobilize beyond providing disenfranchised populations with direct services. Advocacy, at its core, seeks to put in place more equitable policies assuring the rights of the poor are not overlooked. Several Bible verses speak eloquently to a God-given mandate for policy advocacy.

> Speak up for those who cannot speak for themselves,
>   for the rights of all who are destitute.
> Speak up and judge fairly;
>   defend the rights of the poor and needy.
>
> Prov. 31:8–9

> How terrible it will be for those who make unfair laws,
>   and those who write laws that make life hard for
>   people.
> They are not fair to the poor,
>   and they rob my people of their rights.
>
> Isa. 10:1–2a NCV

> This is the kind of fast I'm after:
> to break the chains of injustice,
> get rid of exploitation in the workplace,
> free the oppressed,
> cancel debts.
>
> Isa. 58:6 Message

> How long will you defend the unjust
>   and show partiality to the wicked?

> Defend the weak and the fatherless;
> uphold the cause of the poor and the oppressed.
> Rescue the weak and the needy;
> deliver them from the hand of the wicked.
>
> Ps. 82:2–4

Christians are called to eliminate laws that perpetuate injustice and to work for laws and policies that ensure equity, particularly for the poor and silent voices within our society.

Christian organizations like Bread for the World and World Relief have long taken the lead on faith-based advocacy; their faithful paradigms are a model for any Christian engaging in education reform and policy advocacy. Bread for the World makes the case for Christ as a model of an individual engaging in policy-based advocacy.

> In the New Testament, Jesus was continually in conflict with religious leaders over the essential meaning of the law. Just treatment of people was at the core of his concern: "Woe to you, scribes and Pharisees, hypocrites! For you tithe mint, dill, and cumin, and have neglected the weightier matters of the law: justice and mercy and faith; it is these you ought to have practiced without neglecting the others" (Matt. 23:23). When Jesus challenged the Pharisees and Sadducees, he was confronting the public policy decision-makers.[5]

And World Relief, an international relief organization, likens the Christian's responsibility to advocate for others to Christ's making the ultimate sacrifice and advocating on our behalf.

> World Relief seeks to follow the example of Christ, who intervenes on our behalf to God, as our advocate. Because of Christ's love and support of us, we receive freedom and eternal life. As Christians we are called to be Christ's ambassadors (2 Cor. 5:20), representing Christ to the world and speaking on His behalf.

184

For this reason, we also defend those who are oppressed, weak and who do not have a voice of their own, whether in Darfur, Burma or the United States, just as Christ defends us.[6]

Humans have long struggled to create societies with inherently equal systems and structures. We've almost always erred on the side of favoring the wealthy and slowly crushing the poor and voiceless. Christians living in the United States are blessed. We can generally voice our opinions without fear of retribution. We have the opportunity to speak up for disenfranchised groups. We ought to use that privilege to advocate for systemic change aligned with God's vision of a more equitable society. World Relief sums up this Christian responsibility quite eloquently.

> In the face of the political, social, and religious institutions of our own time, we are likewise called by the Spirit to pray, open our hearts to God, reach out to others in their need, and confront structures, behavior and policies that impoverish and oppress. We are blessed with a system of government that allows us to have a voice in public policy decision. It is legitimate, even imperative, for us to exercise our prophetic ministry in the public policy arena secure in the belief that this is how the Bible directs us.[7]

Moving beyond the Advocacy Barrier

Though one can make a pragmatic and biblical case for education policy advocacy, some Christians and faith leaders remain hesitant about moving into this arena. Through my numerous conversations with clergy and people of faith, I believe the reluctance hinges on a few key issues. I've had the opportunity to "road test" these potential barriers in workshops around the country; faith leaders have helped refine the list to provide a better understanding of what may hinder some people of faith from delving into education reform.

Appearing Too Political

Once we frame education issues in the context of "policy," we shouldn't be surprised that some pastors and clergy appear hesitant. Clergy are legally bound to operate in a strictly apolitical context if they want to keep their tax-exempt status. And for many folks, policy equals political. And that's true to a certain extent. However, advocacy doesn't necessarily need to cross the line into definitive political activities. Congregations and clergy can advocate for particular education reform without campaigning for a particular political candidate who may support a specific education policy. The latter action—explicitly campaigning for a particular candidate or encouraging their membership to vote—is in violation of our nation's Internal Revenue Service restrictions.

But there are plenty of other ways churches can influence education reform! Congregations can host awareness-building events and invite education experts, teachers, and policy makers to discuss various components of education reform issues. Clergy can educate and inform members about education-related legislation or local school board decisions without taking an explicit policy stand. For example, the IRS states:

> Organizations may, however, involve themselves in issues of public policy without the activity being considered as lobbying. For example, organizations may conduct educational meetings, prepare and distribute educational materials, or otherwise consider public policy issues in an educational manner without jeopardizing their tax-exempt status.[8]

The IRS has significant resources for churches and other faith-based organizations that want to understand how they can weigh in on education policy. While there is room to engage, there are certainly limits. Any church or faith-based organization wishing to engage in education policy advocacy should consult the Internal Revenue Service or an attorney specializing in tax-exempt organizations before proceeding.

Pastors and church leaders are not the only people of faith for whom the seemingly "political" nature of education reform presents a stumbling block. Individual Christians may also resist the notion of engaging in anything resembling politics; for some people of faith the idea of moving into an arena governed by state legislators, members of Congress, or other elected officials may be uncomfortable.

I concede that some Christians may never be fully comfortable with advocacy. But we can positively influence other Christians to take action if they are interested, yet apprehensive about politicization. We can connect the policy to the personal, thereby connecting education reform to children rather than political leaders. We can help Christians understand how faith communities have long engaged in advocacy that ultimately helped change laws. Faith-based advocates played a significant role in ending slavery in the United States, forcing desegregation and, hopefully, ensuring all children in our country receive a high-quality education.

Meeting Today's Needs

Creating education policies that are more favorable to students in low-income public schools will not happen overnight. In some cases it can take months or even years. Although the victories are glorious and can revolutionize schooling for thousands of children, sometimes advocates face a long, challenging slog to achieve the prize. I don't mean to be a wet blanket, but I believe realistic expectations help sustain us on the road to long-term change.

Human nature tends to favor instant gratification over protracted (and ever-evolving) legislative battles. People of faith are no exception. Many churches operate direct service ministries to perform the noble and important work of feeding the hungry, clothing the poor, and providing shelter for the homeless. While this work faces its own unique set of challenges and struggles, I suggest that the comfort of feeding a hungry stomach a warm meal allows the meal giver to feel a sense of "right now" joy.

As an interesting contrast, however, I've spoken to Christians who've been involved in direct service ministry for an extended period of time. Almost all of these folks have told me, "It's great that we provided (*fill in the blank with any short-term social need*). But I don't know how they're going to survive tomorrow, next week, or next year. We need to change the structure that perpetuates this problem." That's the power of advocacy and policy reform. We must help Christians understand the long-term and wide-reaching impact of effective education reform. Thousands of students can have more-effective teachers in their classrooms. Tens of thousands of parents can easily receive school achievement information and become more powerful advocates for their children.

We need both short-term and long-term change to improve our nation's schools. As a good friend of mine puts it, "It's great to give backpacks to kids in needy schools. But I don't just want to stop there. Because if those same kids still cannot read at the level of kids in wealthier neighborhoods, what's the point? We also need to give our time and resources to figure out how to close the achievement gap for kids at that school and children in the entire school district. I want to help change the systems and structures to bring *that* type of comprehensive change."

188

Making Enemies

If Christians begin to speak out about education policy and advocate for particular positions, we can potentially alienate those at the other end of the spectrum. I get it. I'm sure some of my friends and colleagues disagree with my opinions about education policy. I may not always like that, but I've become comfortable speaking up for my deep convictions and beliefs. Taking a stand always requires courage. Anyone wanting to confront systemic inequities through advocacy should be prepared for that.

Having said that, I do think we can minimize the number of irate enemies we produce if we operate thoughtfully and respectfully. As a person of faith who strives to model Christlike principles, I try to voice my opinions while balancing confidence and a healthy dose of humility (and I admit the struggle for equilibrium is a continual work in progress). I may disagree with some educators, researchers, or policymakers, but that doesn't mean I should automatically declare that the other camp "doesn't care about children." I will do my best to listen to and understand different perspectives, and then I will take a strong stand on what I believe will best eliminate the academic achievement gap.

Overcoming resistance to education reform and advocacy may require some investment. I encourage any clergy member, faith-based leader, or person of faith considering a systemic approach to education reform to just wade on in. It's not so bad. In fact, you can potentially impact thousands of children in low-income public schools. And you just might be able to convince others to follow you.

Where Can Christians Engage?

The education policy landscape is complex, and anyone, including people of faith, may struggle to identify where they might engage. Every individual, congregation, and organization will need to identify policies of interest and relevance and pinpoint places where they believe they can have a significant impact. I recommend that people of faith advocate for policies where a "moral voice" will offer a particularly unique perspective.

We won't be able to fully explore each of these policy areas in this book, but this section will highlight several education reform areas ripe with opportunity for Christians to get involved. At the end of this section, I propose a series of reflection questions that Christians can begin to explore and discuss—pertaining to their own school district or state (since many education policy decisions happen at the state level). For those who do not live in communities with large populations of low-income families, I recommend identifying a nearby community with large concentrations of low-income families and answer the reflection questions about that area.

Teachers Matter

When I was in elementary and middle school, I waited with anticipation for the first day of seventh grade. That was when we got *her* . . . Mrs. Scharfenberg. She was the one we were waiting for, a true legend. Throughout my twenty-two years of school—primary school, secondary school, undergraduate and graduate studies—Mrs. Scharfenberg is the finest teacher I've ever had. She found a way to motivate all students to become grammar enthusiasts, to get impassioned about Greek mythology, and to strive to learn every botany and biology concept our brains would allow. She challenged us in every way; she set high expectations and we clawed our way to meet them. Mrs. Scharfenberg demonstrated the unique ability to genuinely care about each of us as individuals—which isn't easy with a room full of junior high school kids.

I wish every teacher in my academic career possessed Mrs. Scharfenberg's teaching skills. Like most of us, I experienced a few shining stars at Mrs. Scharfenberg's level. Most of my teachers were solid, and a few, unfortunately, were not very good. While I was already academically motivated, I do know that the quality of my teacher influenced both my interest and my academic outcomes in any given year.

While most teachers work incredibly hard and have the best intentions, teaching is extremely difficult. Some educators are better than others. Certain teachers experience a steeper learning curve and need more professional support. Every teacher can improve. And I know we don't like to admit this, but a small number of educators have probably picked the wrong profession altogether.

Research studies overwhelmingly suggest what most of us know intuitively: quality teachers significantly impact student achievement. Teachers are the single most important "within-school" factor that determines how much a student learns in any given year.[9] For students in low-income communities, many of whom are more than three grade levels behind their peers in wealthier neighborhoods, a high-quality teacher takes on life-altering significance. We have a moral imperative to recruit, prepare, and professionally support teachers in every school, but we must create policies and practices that ensure children who face the challenges associated with poverty have the best teachers possible.

I encourage Christians to consider the following questions as they begin to identify how to engage in teacher quality reform issues.

- What is the process for recruiting and hiring new teachers in my district/state? Does this process work well, or do we see significant teacher shortages or classrooms filled with long-term substitute teachers?

- How does our district/state evaluate teachers?
- How does our district/state reward highly effective teachers?
- How do we determine if a teacher is not as effective as he or she could be? What type of professional development do those teachers receive? What ultimately happens to those teachers?

Informing and Empowering Parents

Whereas teachers are one of the most important in-school factors impacting student achievement, parents are generally identified as the most important "nonschool" influence. Again, this is likely an idea that most people believe intuitively. Parent-power movements have begun to spring up in education reform communities, as more of us realize how futile it is to attempt to improve low-income public schools without engaging parents. Organizations like Parent Revolution and Families for Excellent Schools have begun to equip and mobilize urban parents to take an even more active role in school improvement.

Parents need access to information about school performance in order to demand transformational change that education reform can bring. States, schools, and school districts must provide parents with thorough, readily available, and easy-to-comprehend information about student achievement so they have a clear picture of what is and isn't working in their child's school and classroom. If state, district, or school policies don't currently support this level of transparency, parents should advocate to get every single piece of data they need.

Churches can work with parents in low-income communities to help them understand their parental rights and how they can best advocate for their child and their neighborhood schools. Ideally, this grassroots work will begin within churches that are situated within low-income neighborhoods. Congregations from wealthier neighborhoods can lend their voices, resources, and political clout.

People of faith can ask the following questions about access to information as they begin to identify potential advocacy opportunities:

- How are students in my community performing on academic tests?
- How does this compare to students at schools that are wealthier or less wealthy than the schools in my community?
- Are particular schools more effective than others? What is happening at those schools that could be replicated at other schools?
- How often do I receive information about my child's academic progress?
- Can I readily compare my child's progress to that of other children in my school, district, and state?
- Can I access the student achievement data from last year for my child's future teachers so I can make an informed decision about which teacher is most effective?

Early Childhood Education

A child's cognitive development from birth to five years significantly impacts her or his long-term academic achievement. Unfortunately, most parents, particularly those in poor urban and rural neighborhoods, do not have access to free, high-quality preschool. People of faith can become powerful advocates for this important foundational reform. A few questions to consider:

- How many children in my district/state attend preschool?
- Does my district/state offer universal (e.g., free for everyone) preschool? If not, what are the biggest hindrances to doing so?

- Can we identify local successful examples of high-quality preschools that change the game for children in low-income communities?

Expanding Options

It's virtually impossible to discuss education reform and not consider school choice. The parent choice debate (e.g., publically subsidized vouchers for private and parochial schools, public charter schools, and open enrollment) will likely rage for years. Given the large percentage of children who attend a local neighborhood public school (over 90 percent), school choice is not a silver bullet to eliminate the academic achievement gap. But school choice is here to stay, and anyone interested in education advocacy should have an understanding of the dynamics at play. Our nation's capital provides an illustrative glimpse at the complexities of primarily assigning students to neighborhood public schools.

District of Columbia Public Schools (DCPS) has always educated a particular group of children extremely well. For decades, public school children in the wealthy, largely White, northwest quadrant of the city have achieved at the highest levels. Mann Elementary School is one such school. Located in one of DC's tiniest neighborhoods, it's among the very top tier of high-performing DC public schools. The surrounding blocks are home to members of the United States Congress, successful lobbyists, and corporate attorneys.

According to 2010 standardized test data, 90 percent of Mann students met or exceeded the grade-level standards in reading—with most reading well above grade level. Mann's math test scores are exceptional; 89 percent of students meet or exceed the bar.[10] The school is a three-time Blue Ribbon School Award recipient from the United States Department of Education, and it regularly ranks as one of the highest-performing elementary schools in the nation. Who knew that DC public school students could achieve at such high levels? Given the district's reputation as a dysfunctional and historically underperforming system (a reputation that, sadly, is not without merit), one could assume that every child in DC's schools is destined for failure.

Mann's student body is 80 percent White. The number of students who are eligible for free or reduced-price lunch (which is the best proxy for identifying students from low-income families) is zero. Mann's active, influential, and wealthy Parent Teacher Association (PTA) chapter ensures the school has abundant resources. Mann's PTA has an aggressive fund-raising campaign, complete with matching donations for "corporations, foundations, or embassies." The PTA's annual auction raises enormous amounts of money for Mann. Families can bid on exciting experiences, such as lunch with DC's mayor, a trip to the Virgin Islands, or a round of golf at the exclusive Congressional Country Club. All the proceeds go directly to the school.

The funding surplus helps ensure that Mann's library is well stocked and that teachers are able to bring in additional paid professionals to help with student learning. Students enjoy the most modern technology, and the school grounds include a brand new sports court and organic, student-run garden.[11]

I certainly don't begrudge any parent who wants to go above and beyond to ensure his or her child has the best education possible. It would be difficult for anyone to argue that these parents should stop supplementing their local public school. I call attention to this school to illustrate the vast academic and economic differences among schools within the same public school district.

But here's where this gets interesting: families must reside in the local Mann Elementary neighborhood to receive the school's exemplary education. While DCPS does allow out-of-boundary students to apply to Mann, it's pretty unlikely that those students will get admitted. Mann's website states, "[Ninety-five] percent of the placements are taken up by in-boundary residents." Other DC residents complete an application and hope to get awarded one of the scarce remaining spots through Mann's annual lottery. The chances of that happening are about on par with getting struck by lightning. Twice.

And lest we think that the most ambitious low-income parents should simply relocate to Mann's neighborhood, let's examine the cost of living in this exclusive DC community. Most four-bedroom homes cost anywhere from 1.5 to 3 million dollars.[12] That price range certainly exceeds the average American's budget. And I believe it's safe to say those sticker prices categorically exclude all 102,000 District of Columbia residents living below the poverty line.[13]

Let's take a thirty-minute drive across the Anacostia River into Southeast Washington, DC. About twenty minutes into our trip, you'll notice that the houses get smaller, the faces get browner, and there isn't a Starbucks in sight. There, in the heart of Southeast DC, we find Garfield Elementary School. While both schools are part of the DCPS system, the contrast between Garfield and Mann is striking—particularly in terms of academic outcomes. Only 19 percent of Garfield's students are proficient readers, compared to 90 percent at Mann. (That's a difference of 71 percentage points for those of you keeping score.) Garfield's math scores also indicate massive gaps: only 16 percent of Garfield students perform at grade level, compared to 86 percent of Mann students.[14]

Garfield's student body is 100 percent African American, and almost all (94 percent) are from low-income families. The PTA does have a chapter at Garfield, but the parents have far less political and economic capital to raise significant additional

196

resources for the school. Several nonprofits have started programs for Garfield students. And while those efforts certainly help, they can do little to match the resources of Mann's well-connected parents.

The same rules apply for school enrollment—you have to live within Garfield's street boundaries to attend the school. But you can buy a three-bedroom home in the area for under $100,000, and many residents rent houses or apartments (many of which are subsidized Section 8 housing). It's safe to assume that this neighborhood and its public school are truly open to anyone.

School Funding Formulas

"Aren't you going to say money is the answer?" asked a slightly irritated gentleman at an event where I'd just finished speaking. "That's what everyone always says. Raise my taxes to give schools and teachers more money, and then we can solve this thing!" he finished.

I paused for a moment and responded, "No, I don't think money is the answer. Money alone is not enough to close the academic achievement gap." I had the small post-conference group's attention after that statement. I went on to explain a principle shared by many education reform leaders: money is necessary, but not sufficient, to improve educational outcomes.

But I was also quick to point out that public school funding models don't necessarily promote equity. I told the small gathering that our country should still address fiscal inequality if we want to ensure all children have a fair shot in public schools. You might wonder, isn't that a contradiction? Isn't this idea at odds with chapter 2, where we delved into the ways in which poverty impacts the achievement gap?

Money matters. But it doesn't explain everything. We can compare the amount of money school districts spend on each student and see that per-pupil expenditures do not necessarily correlate with higher achievement. That being said, many school funding formulas are inherently unequal. States provide about 48 percent of school budgets by drawing from corporate taxes, sales taxes, and income taxes. The federal government contributes approximately 8 percent of state education budgets. Local districts contribute about 44 percent, mostly from local property taxes.[15] Altogether, these funds are distributed to school districts on a per-pupil basis (to ensure there is enough to cover each child's education) and categorically (to ensure there is enough for each special program or facility).

In case you missed it, let me highlight the inequity: almost half (44 percent) of school funding comes from local municipalities' property taxes. Wealthier communities generate far greater income from property taxes than poor neighborhoods could ever contribute—so their schools receive significantly more money. Some states have put in "compensation plans" to counter this inequity (e.g., wealthier districts and counties contribute some of their property tax revenue to poorer communities, which offsets some of the funding gap).

Again, while money isn't a differentiator that determines whether a school district can close the achievement gap, we do know that highly successful schools in low-income communities share some common traits. Some of those effective strategies do require more money: extending the school day or school year, increasing salaries for highly effective teachers, and using technology to differentiate student learning.

I'm Ready . . . What Now?

Okay, you may be saying. I surrender! I'm ready to identify specific public education policy issues that can really improve things for children in low-income public schools. Once congregations or a group of Christians assess the policies in their own communities or in low-income neighborhoods near their schools, they can begin to determine how they want to engage.

I recommend building a community of like-minded people, churches, or faith-based organizations and get to work collaboratively. Contact education advocacy organizations, such as The Expectations Project, Stand for Children, or 50CAN, to acquire additional resources and to understand local education issues in your state or school district. From there you can work with advocacy organizations to determine where you can plug into existing advocacy campaigns or help launch your own.

I promise that you won't be disappointed! You may galvanize your fellow Christians to write dozens of emails and letters to elected officials encouraging them to solve a particular issue impacting children in low-income public schools. Or perhaps you'll help get hundreds of thousands of people of faith to attend a rally or an event in support of transformative education reform. Maybe you'll get your pastor to write an op-ed for a local newspaper, calling for a moral voice in public education reform. In any case, you can help our nation get one step closer to its promise of quality public schools for every child.

10

Never Again

Having heard all of this you may choose to look the other way, but you can never again say that you did not know.

—William Wilberforce

During the end of my first year of teaching, my students and I got an unexpected week off from school. The entire nation came to a screeching halt after three White and one Hispanic Los Angeles police officers were acquitted of beating African American motorist Rodney King. The beating, captured on video, garnered worldwide attention. Everyone, myself included, assumed that King's case was a slam-dunk to secure a conviction. The jury's decision set off a literal firestorm in Los Angeles.

I recall sitting in the living room of the Los Angeles home I shared with my two roommates, glued to the television as the historic day unfolded. Vivid images flashed across the screen showing citizens, enraged by the acquittal, looting stores in South

Central Los Angeles; torched businesses and restaurants were engulfed in flames. My roommates and I wept as we watched live footage of the now tragically famous unarmed White truck driver, Reginald Denny, driving unknowingly into a riotous mob and being beaten nearly to death.

I lived about thirty minutes north of Compton. Terrified for the safety of my students, whose homes were in the midst of some of the most violent uprising, I tried to contact as many families as I could. Communication was difficult, so I was left mostly to worry and pray.

As the urban uprising spread north, we watched the looters pillage the Radio Shack, the Subway restaurant, and the grocery store across the street from our house. We quickly packed our bags and hightailed it out of town to stay with a friend about an hour outside of Los Angeles. For the next two days I took refuge in the upscale cocoon of Calabasas; the lush manicured lawns were a stark contrast to news footage of the National Guard and firefighters attempting to extinguish the uprising happening in my students' neighborhood. I felt a strange mixture of relief and guilt as I thought about my students and their families.

School reopened the following Monday, and I made my way back to Compton. The neighborhood streets, which were sparse on business and greenery prior to the uprising, were now dotted with smoldering buildings and burned-out remains of laundromats, fast-food restaurants, nail salons, and liquor stores.

My students seemed happy to return to school. Like every other teacher in the Los Angeles area, I spent most of that first morning processing what happened with my students. A few veteran teachers identified some educational and counseling resources that we could use to help our children cope with everything they'd seen, heard, and experienced the last few days. More than one child cried either openly or privately to me throughout that week. We got into intense discussions about what set things off in the African American community; why people choose to burn and loot businesses in their own neighborhoods; and whether or not it was okay to steal basic necessities like milk or diapers when no grocery stores remained open.

I was most struck by the realization that none of my students left Compton during the uprising. They all talked about the uprising with a firsthand lens. When several students asked me to share my experiences about my neighborhood, I told them that violence did erupt near my community, and I left to stay with friends outside of the city. One earnest student remarked, "That must have been nice to leave, Ms. Baker. We couldn't go anywhere. We were stuck."

We were stuck. Those three simple words still haunt me today. We were stuck. I had the privilege and ability to leave my neighborhood when the Los Angeles uprising got too close for comfort. For various reasons, my students didn't have any other options. Perhaps it was lack of transportation or no relatives or friends outside of the violence zone who would put them up for a few days. Or maybe they didn't leave in time and felt it was too dangerous to take their families on the road during the height of the violence. Whatever the reason, they were stuck. And I wasn't.

I feel the same way about students in low-income public schools with regard to fulfilling their God-given academic potential. Students from families with greater wealth, access, and privilege are not stuck with negative, life-altering educational options. Most students in low-income public schools do not have any alternatives. We need to help provide those options. We need to get them unstuck.

In spite of the challenge and seemingly insurmountable odds, I am hopeful. I am optimistic that we can address America's vast injustice in our public school system. In order to accomplish this goal, we need new, strong moral voices to stand up for children in low-income communities. We need people of faith who live in low-income communities to continue to fight for change in their children's schools. We need pastors and clergy—with congregations in the inner city, the suburbs, and rural communities—to leverage their pulpits to speak against the massive inequities in our nation's public schools.

Now is the time for Christians and all people of faith to become passionate advocates who will ensure all children in this country have the opportunities they deserve. The Christian community can fully embrace our role as vision casters who educate others and ourselves about the challenges and possibilities inherent in our nation's academic achievement gap. Christians can become action-oriented laborers improving education in their local communities by supporting high-quality education nonprofits, tutoring children in low-income schools, and determining the most effective way to partner with public schools. Finally, Christians have a strong and powerful advocacy voice. We can join the education reform debate advocating for policies that will truly close the achievement gap; we can stand for moral, equitable educational policies that help kids in our schools, instead of reinforcing the status quo.

If the United States wants to remain globally competitive, we need to ensure that all students are achieving at high levels. Likewise, if people of faith want to remain relevant to a broken world that is riddled with deep problems, we need to help solve challenges such as the massive inequities in public school students' achievement outcomes. Public school reform also provides opportunities for interfaith collaboration. Each major faith tradition—Christianity, Judaism, Buddhism, Hinduism, and Islam—has core tenets that advocate social responsibility, serving others, and working toward the common good. Public education reform is one of our country's most pressing issues. If we're going to solve this problem, we need Christians, and all people of faith, to be a part of the solution.

And a Child Shall Lead Them

Our youngest daughter's pre-kindergarten class recently had an interesting topic for show-and-tell. Every child had to bring an object that represented his or her parent's occupation. That's a wonderful idea if you're a doctor (send in a stethoscope) or a judge (put a gavel in your kid's backpack). But it's a little tricky when you do what I do. We'd talked about my job before, so my daughter had a basic idea of what I did every day. As we discussed this over dinner, she came up with a plan.

My little daughter got out her drawing tablet and her bag of crayons. And she carefully drew a picture of two schools—one had cracked windows and was very small, and the stick figure kids had sad faces. The other one was expansive, new, and pretty (which in her mind meant that it had pink and purple curtains). The kids at this school had huge smiling faces. She drew a picture of Mommy in the middle of the two schools. On the back of the picture she dictated the words that she would read to her class the next morning: "My mommy helps kids have good schools. Some kids have great schools and other kids don't. I don't think that's fair. So my mommy goes to meetings, talks on the phone, does writing, and makes speeches. She just wants every kid in America to have a good school."

I couldn't have said it any better myself. As Christians, united through our faith and motivated to transform education for all God's children, let's work tirelessly to ensure every child in America has an excellent school.

Additional Resources

The Expectations Project

www.theexpectationsproject.org

A network of faith-based advocates working to close the achievement gap in low-income public schools. Nicole Baker Fulgham is the president and founder.

Teaching

Harlem Children's Zone

www.hcz.org

HCZ has offered educational, social-service, and community-building programs to children and families since 1970. They work with families and students in early childhood, elementary school, middle school, high school, and college.

Memphis Teacher Residency

www.memphistr.org

The mission of the MTR is to positively impact student achievement in Memphis's urban public schools by recruiting, training, and supporting outstanding teachers, all within a Christian context.

The New Teacher Project

www.tntp.org

> The New Teacher Project is a national nonprofit committed to ending the injustice of educational inequality. This organization works with schools, districts, and states to provide excellent teachers to the students who need them most, and to advance policies and practices that ensure effective teaching in every classroom. A large percentage of their participants are mid-career professionals who seek an alternative certification pathway into the classroom.

TEACH.org

www.teach.org

> A national clearinghouse for information about becoming a public school teacher. This comprehensive web portal can help users identify the necessary steps to earning a teaching certificate in any of the fifty states.

Teach For America

www.teachforamerica.org

> Teach For America recruits a diverse group of leaders with a record of achievement who work to expand educational opportunity, starting by teaching for two years in a low-income community. The organization provides intensive training, support, and career development that helps these leaders increase their impact and deepen their understanding of what it takes to close the achievement gap. This growing movement of leaders works at every level of education, policy, and other professions to ensure that all children can receive an excellent education.

Teaching As Leadership

www.teachingasleadership.org

> Teaching As Leadership, a division of Teach For America, explores distinguishing strategies of highly effective teachers

208

to help current and future teachers. Strategies they promote include: set big goals, plan purposefully, execute effectively, continually increase effectiveness, and identify root causes of problems.

Urban Prep Academies

www.urbanprep.org

The mission of Urban Prep is to provide a comprehensive, high-quality college preparatory education to young men that results in their graduates succeeding in college. Urban Prep Academies are African American male public charter schools. Beginning with their first high school graduating class in 2010, every graduate has been accepted into a college or university.

Urban Teacher Residency

www.utr.org

Urban Teacher Residency United (UTRU) serves a growing national network of innovative teacher preparation programs. Founded in 2007, UTRU works closely with school districts, not-for-profit organizations, and universities to launch and support effective training for urban teachers. Based on the medical residency model, Urban Teacher Residencies are district-based education programs that pair master's-level education coursework with a rigorous full-year classroom apprenticeship under the guidance of an experienced mentor teacher.

Mentoring/Adopting a School

20/20 Vision for Schools

www.2020schools.org

20/20 Vision for Schools exists in New York City to transform public schools within a single generation of students.

They achieve this by mobilizing students and community stakeholders to partner with schools for sustainable change.

America's Promise

www.americaspromise.org

> With more than four hundred national partner organizations and their local affiliates, America's Promise is uniquely positioned to mobilize Americans to act. The organization's top priority is ensuring that all young people graduate from high school ready for college, work, and life through the Grad Nation movement. Their work involves raising awareness, creating connections, and sharing knowledge to provide children these five key supports: caring adults, safe places, a healthy start, an effective education, and opportunities to help others.

Communities In Schools

www.communitiesinschools.org

> Communities In Schools began in the 1970s, when Founder Bill Milliken, then a youth advocate in New York City, came up with the idea of bringing community resources inside a public school building—where they are accessible, coordinated, and accountable. In little more than thirty years, Communities In Schools has become the nation's leading dropout prevention organization. It has a unique model that positions a coordinator inside schools to assess needs and deliver necessary resources that remove barriers to success.

DonorsChoose

www.donorschoose.org

> DonorsChoose engages the "public" in public schools by giving people a simple, accountable, and personal way to address educational inequity. Donors can give as little as one dollar to a project request posted on the website by a public school teacher. DonorsChoose.org then purchases

the materials requested and ships them to the classroom in need.

Faith for Change

www.faithforchange.org

Faith for Change is a growing coalition of houses of faith across the country united by a desire and calling to improve academic outcomes for underperforming and high-needs public school students from pre-kindergarten to twelfth grade. Through the Community School Model, educational reform, and programming resources, the coalition hopes to bring about academic success for all students. Faith for Change is a community foundation operating under the Institute for Educational Leadership.

Kids Hope USA

www.kidshopeusa.org

KHUSA offers churches and schools a proven, award-winning model to meet the emotional, social, and academic needs of children. KHUSA programs create one-on-one mentoring relationships between adult church members, willing to give a little time and a lot of love, and at-risk elementary school children in their community who desperately need loving, caring adults in their lives. Utilizing the existing structures of churches and elementary schools as the framework for these programs, Kids Hope USA creates successful, sustainable, and life-changing church-school partnerships.

National Church Adopt-a-School Initiative

www.churchadoptaschool.org

In 2006 the National Church Adopt-a-School Initiative was officially formed to both train and equip churches to replicate Dr. Tony Evans's proven model of social outreach in their area. NCAASI promotes community revitalization through church-based social services by leveraging the existing structures of both churches and schools.

Policy Advocacy

50Can

www.50can.org

The 50-State Campaign for Achievement Now identifies and supports local leaders building movements within their states to make sure that every child has access to a great public school. Their model is built around the conviction that all politics is local but locals shouldn't have to start from scratch. By empowering local leaders, they help create a true, lasting, successful state-based education reform tackling fifty sets of education policy challenges in fifty states to close the achievement gap between the haves and have-nots in America. 50Can supports local leaders to run results-oriented advocacy campaigns through research and policy, communications and mobilization, and advocacy for policy change.

The Center for Education Reform

www.edreform.com

The Center for Education Reform's guiding purpose is to improve the accuracy and quality of discourse and decisions about education reform, leading to fundamental policy changes that make a difference long after news and election cycles have ended. As part of its core mission, the center works on three primary fronts: generating and sharing leading ideas and information, supporting and enabling grassroots activism, and protecting and stimulating media coverage and issue accuracy.

The Center for Faith-based and Neighborhood Partnerships

US Department of Education

www2.ed.gov/about/inits/list/fbci

The mission of the Center for Faith-based and Neighborhood Partnerships at the US Department of Education is to promote student achievement by connecting schools and community-based organizations, both secular and faith-based. The center is part of the White House Office of Faith-based and Neighborhood Partnerships, which works to form partnerships between government at all levels and nonprofit organizations, both secular and faith-based, to more effectively serve Americans in need.

Children's Defense Fund

www.childrensdefense.org

The Children's Defense Fund (CDF) is a non-profit child advocacy organization that has worked relentlessly for nearly 40 years to ensure a level playing field for all children. CDF champions policies and programs that lift children out of poverty; protect them from abuse and neglect; and ensure their access to health care, quality education, and a moral and spiritual foundation. The organization has a long history of successfully working with faith-based organizations

The Education Trust

www.edtrust.org

The Education Trust speaks up for *students,* especially those whose needs and potential are often overlooked. They evaluate every policy, every practice, and every dollar spent through a single lens: what is right for students. They carry out their mission in three primary ways: working alongside educators, parents, students, policymakers, and civic and business leaders in communities across the country, providing practical assistance in their efforts to transform schools and colleges into institutions that serve all students well; analyzing local, state, and national data and using what they learn to help build broader understanding of achievement and opportunity gaps and the actions necessary to close them; and participating actively in national and state policy debates, bringing lessons learned from on-the-ground work and from unflinching data analyses to build the case for policies that will help all students and schools reach high levels of achievement.

Council of Great City Schools

www.cgcs.org

This organization is a member-based coalition of the nation's largest urban public school district. Through their research, policy analysis and legislative agenda CGCS strives to attain three goals: to educate all urban school students to the highest academic standards; to lead, govern and manage our urban public schools in ways that advance the education of our children and inspire the public's confidence; and to engage parents and build a confident, committed and supportive urban community for raising the achievement of urban public schoolchildren.

Families for Excellent Schools

www.familiesforexcellentschools.org

Families for Excellent Schools is a non-profit grassroots organization that works to build a movement of schools and their families in support of every parent's right to choose an excellent school for their child.

National Urban League

www.nul.iamempowered.com

The National Urban League, founded in 1910, has a long history as one of the premier African American civil rights organizations. Their Education and Youth Development division develops innovative programs to support academic achievement, civic involvement, and the physical and emotional development of children and youth. For more than 50 years, the National Urban League has worked to improve educational opportunities for African American students. NUL achieves its goal of fostering academic excellence through the development of policies and programs that focus on early childhood education, college preparedness, and youth leadership programs.

Parent Revolution

www.parentrevolution.org

The Parent Revolution team works directly with parents at underperforming schools in Los Angeles and throughout California to help parents organize to transform their children's underperforming schools using California's historic Parent Trigger law. They use sophisticated and cutting-edge community organizing techniques to help parents organize, create Parents Union chapters, build power, analyze their school's performance, and fight for kids-first reforms that will dramatically improve academic outcomes for their children.

Stand for Children

www.stand.org

Stand for Children's mission is to ensure that all children, regardless of background, graduate from high school prepared for, and with access to, a college education. To make this happen, it educates and empowers parents, teachers, and community members to demand excellent public schools; advocates for effective local, state, and national education policies and investments; ensures the policies and funding they advocate for reach classrooms and help students; and elects courageous leaders who will stand up for their priorities.

Students for Education Reform

www.studentsforedreform.org

With thousands of members across the country, SFER is creating a vibrant, fast-growing movement of students fighting to close the racial and socioeconomic achievement gap in public schools across the United States. On campus, chapter leaders are responsible for building a small, effective leadership team; developing young leaders to come behind them; increasing campus awareness of the achievement gap and need for systemic reform; creating a campus coalition for education reform that includes minority affinity and social justice groups; placing students in internships with mission-aligned organizations; and turning out undergraduates in support of ambitious, pro-student legislation.

StudentsFirst

www.studentsfirst.org

StudentsFirst formed in 2010 in response to an increasing demand for a better education system in America. This grassroots movement is designed to mobilize parents, teachers, students, administrators, and citizens throughout the country, and to channel their energy to produce meaningful results on both the national and local levels.

Books

Savage Inequalities, by Jonathan Kozol

Kozol's book paints probably one of the most heartbreaking and accurate portrayals of the vast inequities in our nation's public schools.

The Black-White Test Score Gap, by Christopher Jencks and Meredith Phillips

The book offers a comprehensive look at the factors that contribute to the Black-White test score gap and discusses options for substantially reducing it. Although significant attempts have been made over the past three decades to shrink the test score gap, including increased funding for predominantly Black schools, desegregation of southern schools, and programs to alleviate poverty, the median Black American still scores below 75 percent of American Whites on most standardized tests. The book brings together recent evidence on some of the most controversial and puzzling aspects of the test score debate, including the roles of test bias, heredity, and family background. It also looks at how and why the gap has changed over the past generation; reviews the educational, psychological, and cultural explanations for the gap; and analyzes its educational and economic consequences.

Unfinished Business: Closing the Racial Achievement Gap in Our Schools, by Pedro Noguera and Jean Yonemura Wing

In this groundbreaking book, coeditors Pedro Noguera and Jean Yonemura Wing and their collaborators investigated the dynamics of race and achievement at Berkeley High School— a large public high school that the *New York Times* called "the most integrated high school in America." Berkeley's diverse student population clearly illustrates the "achievement gap" phenomenon in our schools. *Unfinished Business* brings to light the hidden inequities of schools—where cultural attitudes, academic tracking, curricular access, and after-school activities serve as sorting mechanisms that set students on paths of success or failure.

A *Chance to Make History*, by Wendy Kopp

Since 1990, Teach For America has been building a movement to end educational inequity in America. Now its founder, Wendy Kopp, shares the lessons learned from the experiences of more than 25,000 teachers and alumni who have taught and led schools in low-income communities during those years. Sharing her experiences in some of the country's most underserved communities, Kopp introduces leaders at the classroom, school, and system levels who, driven by passionate belief in their students' potential, have set out to accomplish what most think impossible. Their inspiring stories show how we can provide children facing all the challenges of poverty with an excellent education, and that doing so involves the same ingredients that account for success in any endeavor: visionary leadership that sets ambitious goals and puts forth the energy and discipline to reach them.

Relentless Pursuit: A Year in the Trenches with Teach For America, by Donna Foote

When Locke High School opened its doors in 1967, the residents of Watts celebrated it as a sign of the changes promised by Los Angeles. But four decades later, first-year Teach For America recruits Rachelle, Phillip, Hrag, and Taylor are greeted by a school that looks more like a prison, with bars, padlocks, and chains all over. With little training and experience, these four will be asked to produce academic gains in students who are among the most disadvantaged in the country. *Relentless Pursuit* lays bare the experiences of these four teachers to evaluate their strengths and challenges.

How It's Being Done: Urgent Lessons from Unexpected Schools, by Karin Chenoweth

How It's Being Done offers much-needed help to educators, providing detailed accounts of the ways in which unexpected schools—those with high-poverty and high-minority student populations—have dramatically boosted student achievement and diminished (and often eliminated) achievement gaps. *How It's Being Done* builds on Karin Chenoweth's widely hailed earlier volume, *It's Being Done*, providing specific information about how such schools have exceeded expectations and met with unprecedented levels of success.

Documentary Films

Ten9Eight: Shoot For the Moon

www.ten9eight.com

Children from urban communities are given the opportunity to compete in a nationwide business plan.

American Teacher

www.theteachersalaryproject.org

This film follows four public school teachers who work in low-income communities, with a focus on their personal financial challenges and other daily struggles.

The Lottery

www.thelotteryfilm.com

In a country where 58 percent of African American fourth-graders are functionally illiterate, *The Lottery* uncovers the failures of the traditional public school system and reveals that hundreds of thousands of parents attempt to flee the system every year. *The Lottery* follows four of these families from Harlem and the Bronx who have entered their children in a charter school lottery. Out of thousands of hopefuls, only a small minority will win the chance of a better future.

Directed by Madeleine Sackler and shot by award-winning cinematographer Wolfgang Held, *The Lottery* uncovers a ferocious debate surrounding the education reform movement. Interviews with politicians and educators explain not only the crisis in public education, but also why it is fixable. A call to action to avert a catastrophe in the education of American children, *The Lottery* makes the case that any child can succeed.

Teached

www.teached.org

These series of short and compelling documentary films illustrate some of the key components of the academic achievement gap and how it impacts students and families. The films begin to identify solutions to some of the most troubling aspects of educational disparity.

UnDivided

www.undivided.themovie.com

A church in suburban Portland, Oregon, develops a meaningful and transformational partnership with an urban public school. The documentary chronicles the lessons learned when forging this important relationship.

Waiting for Superman

www.waitingforsuperman.com

Waiting for Superman is a 2010 documentary film from director Davis Guggenheim. The film analyzes the failures of American public education by following several students through the educational system, who hope to be selected in a lottery for some of the highest-performing public charter schools.

While this film does present a heavy-handed and somewhat simplistic perspective about the evils of teachers unions, the overall documentary does poignantly illustrate the vast inequities in American public schools.

Acknowledgments

Like most books, this work was not completed on an island; the list of people who supported this project goes on for quite a while.

I am very fortunate to have this project guided by the amazing staff at Baker Publishing and Brazos Press. Bob Hosack, Bobbi Jo Heyboer, Trinity Graeser, Jim Kinney, Jeremy Wells, Brian Dyer, and Paula Gibon have all supported this book and encouraged me throughout the process. A huge shout-out goes to Lisa Ann Cockrel (editor extraordinaire!) and her fabulous team: Barbara Dick and Susan Matheson. You all helped me gain an entirely new appreciation for what it takes to get a book ready to publish!

An extra-special thanks to every teacher, faith-based leader, and pastor who let me interview him or her for this book. You all are incredibly busy people, and I'm beyond grateful that you took the time to share your stories with me. To my two fabulous American Studies Program interns, Rachel Plourde and Rebecca Schofstall, thanks for all of your research, editing, and encouragement. To my Teach For America colleagues,

Jason Kloth, Josh Dickson, Tracy-Elizabeth Clay, Shani Jackson Dowell, Daniel Grant, Rebecca Neale, and Brandon Sammut, you have all contributed to this book in numerous ways. A special note of thanks goes to Wendy Kopp, Kevin Huffman, Elissa Kim, and Matt Kramer for supporting Teach For America's faith community outreach initiative, which ultimately led me to this book project.

My girlfriends Constance Renee, Kimberly, Adrienne, Karen, Carrie, Angela, and Michele continuously encouraged me, prayed for me, got me out of the house when I needed a writing break, and listened to my probably-quite-boring rants about chapter edits, endnotes, and other mundane topics. I am grateful for true friends. You all are the best!

A host of other people have been helpful in various ways along this journey: Wes Moore, Leith Anderson, Jim Wallis, Debbie Kavorcus, Marshall Mitchell, Carol Johnson, Terry Carter, Mike Flaherty, and Tim King. If I've omitted anyone, please attribute it to my head and faulty memory . . . not my lack of gratitude.

To my mom and dad, who were my very first teachers: It's nearly impossible to find adequate words to thank the two people who quite literally gave me life, taught me how to read, made sure I succeeded in school, and sacrificed to ensure I received the best education possible. If I am even half the parent you have been, our children will be immensely blessed.

For our children: To Jacqueline, thank you for being one of the first people to read any portion of this book and for encouraging me (and for laughing in the right places!). To Travis, when I felt stressed out in the throes of trying to complete this book, your incredible wit and humor helped me stay sane when I needed a mental break from writing. And to Mackenzie, my littlest bean, your joyous smile and loving personality continually inspire me. You can do a happy dance now that Mommy's book is done!

To my husband, Alonzo: Thank you for your immeasurable support and unconditional love during this process. I am grateful for your limitless encouragement (you truly believed in this book even before I wrote one single word) and for keeping our family intact during numerous weekend and late-night writing sessions. I could not have done this without you. I'll forever strive to be as supportive to you as you've been to me.

Finally, any good thing that results from this book has to be credited to the One who inspired this work. I am amazed that God has allowed me to speak on behalf of his children, even in this small way.

Notes

Chapter 1 A School System Deeply Divided

1. Most school districts primarily assign students to their local public school based on neighborhood boundaries. Detroit, like many school districts, has a small percentage of open enrollment schools. These magnet schools tend to have long waiting lists or use a lottery process to determine admittance.

2. Public school integration became mandatory after the Supreme Court's 1954 ruling (*Brown v. Board of Education*). As desegregation laws were put in place, during the late 1960s and early 1970s, White families moved out of cities in droves. This demographic shift created what researchers have called de facto segregation. Racially segregated neighborhoods, by default, re-create public school segregation.

3. The names of all personal friends have been changed, unless otherwise noted.

4. The names of students, fellow teachers, and the school where I taught have all been changed.

5. "School Accountability Report Cards," Axiom Management Advisors and Consultants, http://www.axiomadvisors.net (accessed November 11, 2011).

6. Karen Diegmeuller, "Academic Deficiencies Force Takeover of California District," *Education Week*, http://www.edweek.org/ew /articles/1992/09/16/02-2comp.h12.html (accessed November 27, 2011).

7. United States Department of Education, National Center for Education Statistics, *The Condition of Education 2009* (NCES 2009–081), Indicator 32.

8. The Editorial Projects in Education Research Center, "Diplomas Count 2011: Beyond High School, before Baccalaureate," *Education Week* 30, no. 34.

9. "Closing the Gaps Data Points," *Education Trust*, October 15, 2009, http://www.edtrust.org/dc/publication/closing-the-gaps-data -points (accessed December 12, 2011).

Chapter 2 Root Causes, Systemic Factors, and Myths

1. For those who want to delve more deeply into the academic achievement gap, and its root causes, I'd recommend two books: Christopher Jencks and Meredith Phillips, *The Black-White Test Score Gap* (Washington, DC: Brookings Institution Press, 1998), and Pedro Noguera and Jean Yonemura Wing, *Unfinished Business: Closing the Racial Achievement Gap in Our Schools* (San Francisco: Jossey-Bass, 2006).

2. Betty Hart and Todd R. Risley, *Meaningful Differences in the Everyday Experience of Young American Children* (Baltimore: PH Brooks, 1995).

3. Institute of Education Sciences, National Assessment of Educational Progress, The Nation's Report Card: Reading 2011, November 2011, http://nces.ed.gov/nationsreportcard/pdf/main2011/2012457.pdf (accessed January 5, 2012).

4. Christopher B. Swanson, *Crisis in Cities: Closing the Graduation Gap*, April 2009, http://www.americaspromise.org/our-work/Dropout -Prevention/~/media/Files/Our%20Work/Dropout%20Prevention /Cities%20in%20Crisis/Cities_In_Crisis_Report_2009.ashx (accessed September 3, 2012).

5. McKinsey & Company, Social Sector Office, *The Economic Impact of the Achievement Gap in America's Schools*, April 2009, 12.

6. *Starting Smart: How Early Experiences Affect Brain Development*, http://main.zerotothree.org/site/DocServer/startingsmart.pdf ?docID=2422 (accessed October 17, 2011).

7. Private preschool admissions have developed into a cottage industry, particularly in New York City. Entire books, websites, and even a documentary film, *Nursery University*, chronicle the preschool admissions competition.

8. United States Department of Health and Human Services, *Head Start Impact Study*, January 2010, www.acf.hhs.gov/programs/opre /hs/impact_study/reports/impact_study/executive_summary_final.pdf (accessed December 17, 2011).

9. Press release from Share Our Strength, http://www.strength.org /press_release/20110914/. Data collected from Alisha Coleman-Jensen et al., *Household Food Security in the United States in 2010*, September 2011, http://www.ers.usda.gov/Publications/ERR125/err125.pdf (accessed December 16, 2011).

10. R. Garg et al., *Asthma Facts, Second Edition*, May 2003, http:// www.nyc.gov/html/doh/downloads/pdf/asthma/facts.pdf (accessed December 22, 2011).

11. Richard Rothstein, "A Look at the Health-Related Causes of Low Student Achievement," *Economic Policy Institute*, March 1, 2011, http://www.epi.org/publication/a_look_at_the_healthrelated_causes_ of_low_student_achievement/ (accessed January 3, 2012).

12. Diane Ravitch is one of the most prominent voices arguing the importance of poverty when trying to eliminate the academic achievement gap. Her most recent book delves into the poverty argument: *The Death and Life of the Great American School System: How Testing and Choice Are Undermining Education* (New York: Basic Books), 2010. Also, see a shorter blog post that summarizes this perspective: Michael Rebell and Jessica Wolff, "U.S. Schools Have a Poverty Crisis, Not an Education Crisis," *Huffington Post*, February 2, 2012, http://www.huffingtonpost.com/michael-rebell/us-schools -have-a-poverty_b_1247635.html (accessed February 2, 2012).

13. Charles V. Willie, "The Social and Historical Context: A Case Study of Philanthropic Assistance" in *The Education of African*

Americans, ed. Charles V. Willie et al. (New York: Auburn House, 1991), 12–13.

14. Charla Bear, "American Indian Boarding Schools Haunt Many," *National Public Radio*, May 12, 2008, www.npr.org/templates/story /story.php?storyId=16516865 (accessed February 1, 2012).

15. William Velez, "Educational Experiences of Hispanics in the United States," in *Handbook of Hispanic Cultures in the United States: Sociology*, ed. Felix Padilla (Houston: Arte Publico Press, 1994), 151–60.

16. Robert Teranishi, *Black Residential Migration in California: Implications for Higher Education Policy*, Research and Policy Institute of California, http://steinhardt.nyu.edu/scmsAdmin/uploads/005/841 /RTT_RPIC.pdf (accessed November 2, 2011).

17. Michelle Fuetsch, "Latino Aspirations on Rise in Compton: Demographics: Latinos Stream into the Area. Some Say the Black-Run City Is Hostile to Their Needs," *Los Angeles Times*, May 7, 1990, http://articles.latimes.com/1990-05-07/local/me-134_1_latino-children (March 17, 2012).

18. For more information about subconscious teacher bias, read the following landmark study of kindergarten teachers in low-income urban schools: Ray Rist, "Harvard Education Review Classic Reprint: Student Social Class and Teacher Expectations: Self-fulfilling Prophecy in Ghetto Education," *Harvard Educational Review* 70, no. 3 (Fall 2000), 257–302.

Chapter 3 The Good News

1. Wendy Kopp, *A Chance to Make History: What Works and What Doesn't in Providing an Excellent Education for All* (New York: PublicAffairs, 2011), 113.

2. President George W. Bush authorized No Child Left Behind in 2001. This landmark piece of legislation required unprecedented state and local standardized testing and, subsequently, a new layer of accountability for educational outcomes.

3. Several articles highlight KIPP schools' successes: Bill Turque, "Report Finds KIPP Students Outscore Public School Peers,"

Washington Post, June 22, 2010, www.washingtonpost.com/wp-dyn /content/article/2010/06/22/AR2010062200009.html; "The Time to Learn: KIPP Schools Show What a Longer School Day Offers," *Washington Post*, July 19, 2010, www.washingtonpost.com/wp-dyn /content/article/2010/07/19/AR2010071904357.html; and Greg Toppo, "Knowledge Is Power Program Shown as Urban Triumph," *USA Today*, February 11, 2009, www.usatoday.com/news/education/2009-02-11 -kipp-knowledge-power_N.htm.

4. IDEA Public Schools Annual Reports, 2007–2011, http://www .ideapublicschools.org/domain/34; (accessed August 31, 2012).

5. "Five IDEA Schools Make NCEA Higher Performing Schools List," *Brownsville Herald*, October 27, 2011, www.brownsvilleherald .com/articles/schools-132939-list-idea.html (accessed June 22, 2012).

6. "Best High Schools: Rankings 2012," *US News & World Report*, http://www.usnews.com/education/best-high-schools/texas/districts /yes-preparatory-public-schools (accessed June 22, 2012).

7. Christine Armario, "Houston's YES Prep Charter Schools Win Broad Prize," *ABC News*, June 21, 2012, http://abcnews.go.com/US/wire Story/houstons-prep-charter-schools-win-broad-prize-16623407#.T -Ua8Ree4l8 (accessed June 22, 2012).

8. Education Trust, *Success Stories*, http://www.edtrust.org/dc /resources/success-stories (accessed August 24, 2012).

9. Kurt Kaiser, "Pass It On," Lexicon Music, 1969.

Chapter 4 A Rich History, An Absent Voice

1. C. S. Lewis, *The Screwtape Letters, with Screwtape Proposes a Toast* (San Francisco: HarperSanFrancisco, 2001).

2. Amy Sullivan, "Young Evangelicals: Expanding Their Mission," *Time*, June 2010, http://www.time.com/time/nation/article /0,8599,1992463,00.html; Francis Fitzgerald, "The New Evangelicals," *New Yorker*, June 30, 2008; Lisa Miller, "The New Evangelical Vote," *Washington Post*, January 5, 2012, http://www.washingtonpost.com /national/on-faith/iowa-caucuses-dispel-the-myth-of-monolithic -narrow-evangelical-voters/2012/01/05/gIQAjbq4eP_story.html (accessed January 6, 2012); Marcia Pally, "The New Evangelicals," *New*

York Times, December 9, 2011, http://campaignstops.blogs.nytimes
.com/2011/12/09/the-new-evangelicals/ (accessed January 6, 2012).

3. Eric Metaxas, *Amazing Grace: William Wilberforce and the Heroic Campaign to End Slavery* (San Francisco: HarperOne, 2007).

4. Stephen Tomkins, *William Wilberforce: A Biography* (Grand Rapids: Eerdmans, 2007).

5. Stephen Tomkins, *The Clapham Sect: How Wilberforce's Circle Changed Britain* (Oxford: Lion, 2010), 192–94.

6. Michael Peters, *Robert Raikes: The Founder of Sunday School 1780* (Enumclaw, WA: Pleasant Word, 2008).

7. Ibid., 42.

8. Ibid., 44.

9. Lyle Dorsett, *A Passion for Souls: The Life of D. L. Moody* (Chicago: Moody Publishing, 2003).

10. James Axtell, *The School upon a Hill: Education and Society in Colonial New England* (New Haven: Yale University Press, 1974).

11. "Educating Our Children," Lutheran Church Missouri Synod, http://www.lcms.org/page.aspx?pid=1163 (accessed September 19, 2011).

12. Jane Buerger, "Go . . . and Teach! Changing Faces in Lutheran Schools: Racial, Ethnic and Cultural Diversity," *Lutheran Education Journal,* December 10, 2010, http://lej.cuchicago.edu/columns/go -...-and-teach-changing-faces-in-lutheran-schools-racial-ethnic-and -cultural-diversity/ (accessed September 19, 2011).

13. For more information on Seton Education Partners, see: www .setonpartners.org.

14. Martin Scanlan, "The Grammar of Catholic Schooling and Radically 'Catholic' Schools," *Catholic Education: A Journal of Inquiry and Practice* 12, no. 1 (September 2008).

15. Ibid.

16. Stephanie Saroki and Christopher Levenick, *Saving America's Urban Catholic Schools: A Guide for Donors* (Washington, DC: Philanthropy Roundtable, 2009).

17. "Seven Themes of Catholic Teaching," United States Conference of Catholic Bishops, http://www.usccb.org/beliefs-and-teachings

/what-we-believe/catholic-social-teaching/seven-themes-of-catholic -social-teaching.cfm (accessed December 17, 2011). Text is drawn from *Sharing Catholic Social Teaching: Challenges and Directions* (Washington, DC: USCCB, 1998) and *Faithful Citizenship: A Catholic Call to Political Responsibility* (Washington, DC: USCCB, 2003).

18. J. M. O'Keefe, "No Margin, No Mission," in *The Contemporary Catholic School: Context, Identity, and Diversity*, ed. T. H. McLaughlin, J. M. O'Keefe, and B. O'Keeffe (Washington, DC: Falmer Press, 1996), 177–97.

19. Congregation for Catholic Education, *The Catholic School* (Washington, DC: United States Catholic Conference, 1977), 58.

20. David Nevin and Robert E. Bills, *The Schools That Fear Built* (Washington, DC: Acropolis Books, 1976).

21. D. Barton, *America: To Pray or Not to Pray* (Aledo, TX: Wall-Builder Press, 1988).

22. S. D. Rose, *Keeping Them Out of the Hands of Satan: Evangelical Schooling in America* (New York: Routledge, 1988).

23. National Center for Education Statistics, "1.5 Million Home-schooled Students in the United States in 2007," http://nces.ed.gov /pubsearch/pubsinfo.asp?pubid=2009030 (accessed February 2, 2012).

Chapter 6 Motivating and Sustaining Faith

1. Teach For America surveys its corps members and alumni on a variety of topics, including religious background or affiliation. These questions are optional and have no bearing on who is admitted into the program. Used with permission from Teach For America, Inc.

2. Texas House Bill 588, generally known as the "Top 10% Rule," passed in 1997. The measure allows automatic college acceptance at Texas state colleges and universities to any student who graduates in the top 10 percent of his or her high school class. The bill was passed as an affirmative action measure that attempted to help students in low-income communities, which is different from the race-based affirmative action policies of the 1970s and 1980s. Critics of the policy argue that it unfairly disadvantages students from higher-achieving high schools (which, on the average, are schools in middle-class and

wealthy communities), where the competition to graduate in the top 10 percent is arguably more challenging. http://en.wikipedia.org/wiki/Texas_House_Bill_588 (accessed November 6, 2011).

3. Amy Sullivan, "Young Evangelicals: Expanding Their Mission," *Time*, June 1, 2010.

4. Jason Amos, *Dropouts, Diplomas and Dollars*, Alliance for Excellent Education, http://www.all4ed.org/files/Econ2008.pdf (accessed December 29, 2011).

Chapter 7 Closing the Awareness Gap

1. Rick Warren, *The Purpose Driven Life: What on Earth Am I Here For?* (Grand Rapids: Zondervan, 2002).

2. Chapters 1–3 of Habakkuk illustrate God's coming judgment on what appears to be a godless nation where, interestingly, injustice (among other sins) reigned.

3. Malcolm Gladwell, *The Tipping Point: How Little Things Can Make a Big Difference* (New York: Back Bay Books, 2000).

4. Jonathan Kozol, *Savage Inequalities: Children in America's Schools* (New York: Harper Perennial, 1992).

5. For additional resources regarding small group discussions about public education and the academic achievement gap, see: www.theexpectationsproject.org.

6. For detailed examples of tools that church leaders can use with sermons and teaching lessons, see: www.theexpectationsproject.org.

7. I recommend viewing *Waiting for Superman* (www.waitingforsuperman.com), *The Lottery* (www.thelotteryfilm.com), or *Won't Back Down* (www.wbdtoolkit.org). All three movies offer great insight into the academic achievement gap. The first two films are documentaries, while *Won't Back Down* portrays a fictionalized version of real life events in which parents and teachers collaborate to turn around a failing school.

8. Wendy Kopp, *One Day All Children: The Unlikely Triumph of Teach For America and What I Learned along the Way* (New York: PublicAffairs, 2001).

9. For more information on Michelle Rhee's organization, StudentsFirst, see www.studentsfirst.org.

10. For more information on the Harlem Children's Zone, see www.hcz.org.

Chapter 8 Laborers in the Movement

1. See the Additional Resources section for a list of teacher training organizations.

2. Memphis Teacher Residency, http://www.memphistr.org/mission (accessed on January 22, 2012).

3. Memphis Teacher Residency, http://www.memphistr.org/what webelieve (accessed on January 22, 2012).

4. Monica Selby, "A Christian Teacher Residency Program That Eschews Classroom Evangelism," *Christianity Today*, January 24, 2012, http://www.christianitytoday.com/thisisourcity/7thcity/class roomevangelism.html (accessed February 11, 2012).

5. See the Additional Resources section for a comprehensive list of key organizations that effectively recruit, train, and support teachers in low-income public schools.

6. Community Partnership School, http://www.haverford.edu/CPGC /files/community_partnership_school.pdf (accessed January 21, 2012).

7. To view the entire video, go to www.wearenotwaiting.com.

8. New Leaders for New Schools, http://www.newleaders.org/impact /results/ (accessed January 21, 2012).

9. The Shrines of the Black Madonna, http://www.theshrineonline .org/kipp-liberation-academy.html (accessed January 22, 2012).

10. Hartford Institute for Religion Research, http://hirr.hartsem .edu/research/fastfacts/fast_facts.html#sizecong (accessed January 22, 2012).

11. The best proxy for high-poverty schools is what the National Center for Education Statistics identifies as Title I schools. Title I is a federally funded program that allocates additional money to schools with high concentrations of children living in poverty. These data were retrieved from: *Numbers and Types of Elementary and Secondary Schools from the Common Core Data: School Year 2009-2010, Table*

2. *Number of operating public elementary and secondary schools, by school type, charter, magnet, Title I, and Title I school wide status, and state or jurisdiction*, http://nces.ed.gov/pubs2011/pesschools09/tables/table_02.asp#f3 (accessed March 1, 2012).

12. For more information on World Impact or The Simple Way, see www.worldimpact.org and www.thesimpleway.org.

13. Amy Julia Becker, "School Choice of a Different Kind," *Christianity Today*, April 2012, vol. 56, no. 4, 22.

14. Ibid.

15. Ibid.

16. The Simple Way, "Frequently Asked Questions," http://www.thesimpleway.org/about/faq (accessed February 1, 2012).

Chapter 9 Faith-Based Advocacy

1. Data gathered from the Ohio Department of Education's school district report cards, http://ilrc.ode.state.oh.us/ (accessed February 9, 2011).

2. "Kelley Williams-Bolar, Ohio Mother, Convicted of Lying to Get Kids in Better Schools," *Huffington Post*, January 27, 2011, http://www.huffingtonpost.com/2011/01/27/kelley-williams-bolar-schools_n_814857.html (accessed February 9, 2011).

3. For a more detailed account of Michelle Rhee's role as chancellor of the DC public schools, see Richard Whitmore, *The Bee Eater: Michelle Rhee Takes on the Nation's Worst School District* (San Francisco: Jossey-Bass, 2011).

4. For more insight into the rancorous debate among education reformers, I recommend two books that detail both sides of the debate pretty succinctly: Steven Brill, *Class Warfare: Inside the Fight to Fix America's Schools* (New York: Simon and Schuster, 2011), and Diane Ravitch, *The Death and Life of the Great American School System: How Testing and Choice Are Undermining Education* (New York: Basic Books, 2010).

5. Bread for the World, "Biblical Basis for Advocacy," http://www.bread.org/hunger/bible/biblical-basis/biblical-basis-for-advocacy.pdf (accessed January 29, 2012).

6. World Relief, "Why Advocate?," http://worldrelief.org/advocate (accessed January 29, 2012).

7. Ibid.

8. Internal Revenue Service, *Charities & Non-Profits: Lobbying*, http://www.irs.gov/charities/article/0,,id=163392,00.html (accessed February 17, 2012).

9. Parent involvement, parents' educational background, and family income level certainly influence student achievement; these factors account for the widest variance in student achievement. Of the "within-school" factors that have been isolated and studied, teacher effectiveness seems to account for the largest differences in student achievement.

10. Horace Mann Elementary School, District of Columbia Public Schools, http://profiles.dcps.dc.gov/Mann+Elementary+School (accessed November 3, 2011).

11. Horace Mann Elementary School, http://www.horancemann.org (accessed November 3, 2011).

12. This estimate was derived from searching www.trulia.com, a national real estate website, during the fall of 2011.

13. U.S. Census Data from 2006–2010, http://quickfacts.census.gov/qfd/states/11000.html (accessed November 17, 2011).

14. "Garfield Elementary School," District of Columbia Public Schools, http://profiles.dcps.dc.gov/Garfield+Elementary+School (accessed January 8, 2011).

15. Bruce D. Baker et al., Is School Funding Fair? A National Report Card, September 2010, http://www.schoolfundingfairness.org/National_Report_Card.pdf (accessed August 30, 2012).

Nicole Baker Fulgham is the founder and president of *The Expectations Project*, a non-profit organization that mobilizes faith-motivated advocates to help close the academic achievement gap in public schools.

A native of Detroit, Nicole graduated from the University of Michigan and taught fifth grade at a public school in Compton, California. Nicole received her PhD in education from UCLA with a focus on urban education policy and teacher preparation. She worked as a researcher and analyst for the Council of Great City Schools. Nicole then joined the national staff of Teach For America, where she held several key leadership roles, including vice president of new site development, vice president of teacher training and support and vice president of faith community relations.

In 2012, Nicole was selected out of more than 3,000 applicants as one of seven recipients of The Mind Trust's Education Entrepreneur Fellowship. She speaks regularly at faith-based and education conferences, has appeared on CNN and ABC News, and authored several articles about educational equity. *Christianity Today* singled Nicole as One to Watch and also named her one of the 50 Women Leaders Influencing the Church and Culture.

Nicole is on the board of several non-profit organizations and community service groups. She lives in the Washington, DC area with her husband and their three children.